£10.75

An Introductory Guide to
Post-structuralism and Postmodernism

By the same author:

Marxism and Education (Routledge & Kegan Paul, 1978)
Education, State and Crisis (Routledge & Kegan Paul, 1982)
Marxism, Structuralism, Education (Falmer Press, 1983)
The Politics of Multiracial Education (Routledge & Kegan Paul, 1986)

An Introductory Guide to Post-structuralism and Postmodernism

Madan Sarup

Goldsmiths' College
University of London

HARVESTER WHEATSHEAF
NEW YORK LONDON TORONTO SYDNEY TOKYO SINGAPORE

First published 1988 by
Harvester Wheatsheaf
66 Wood Lane End, Hemel Hempstead
Hertfordshire HP2 4RG
A division of
Simon & Schuster International Group

Printed and bound in Great Britain by
Billing & Sons Ltd, Worcester

British Library Cataloguing in Publication Data

Sarup, Madan
An introductory guide to post-structuralism and
postmodernism.
1. European philosophy
I. Title
190
ISBN 0-7108-1339-2
ISBN 0-7108-1349-X Pbk

4 5   92 91

For Sita in reparation

Contents

Acknowledgements   viii

Introduction   1

Chapter 1   Lacan and psychoanalysis   6

Chapter 2   Derrida and deconstruction   34

Chapter 3   Foucault and the social sciences   63

Chapter 4   Some currents within post-structuralism   96

Chapter 5   Postmodernism   117

Conclusion   141

Notes   152

Notes on Further Reading   162

Index   169

Acknowledgements

My students at Goldsmiths' College wanted a short, accessible account that made links between the many discourses—philosophy, psychoanalysis, literature, the social sciences, politics, art—that are usually taught in isolation. I would like to thank them for encouraging me to write this textbook. I have drawn on the work of many people—all writing is intertextual—and they are acknowledged in the *Notes*. For intellectual stimulus and emotional support I would like to thank Elza Adamowicz, John Colbeck, Peter Dunwoodie, Eileen Jebb, Anne Kampendonk, Paul Maltby, Tasneem Raja and many others. I am particularly grateful to Bernard Burgoyne and Peter Dews, from whom I have learnt so much.

Introduction

During the last thirty years or so the structuralists and post-structuralists have made some very important contributions to human understanding. Lévi-Strauss, Lacan, Derrida, Foucault, Deleuze, Lyotard have produced an impressive body of work. Though structuralism and post-structuralism are very different—the latter theory, for example, does not use structural linguistics in its work—there are some similarities: both approaches make critiques.

Firstly, there is a *critique of the human subject*. The term 'subject' refers to something quite different from the more familiar term 'individual'. The latter term dates from the Renaissance and presupposes that man is a free, intellectual agent and that thinking processes are not coerced by historical or cultural circumstances. This view of Reason is expressed in Descartes's philosophical work. Consider this phrase: 'I think, therefore I am.' Descartes's 'I' assumes itself to be fully conscious, and hence self-knowable. It is not only autonomous but coherent; the notion of another psychic territory, in contradiction to consciousness, is unimaginable. In his work Descartes offers us a narrator who imagines that he speaks without simultaneously being spoken.

Lévi-Strauss, a leading structuralist, called the human subject—the centre of being—the 'spoilt brat of philosophy'. He stated that the ultimate goal of the human sciences is not to constitute man but to dissolve him. This became the slogan of structuralism. The leading philosopher of the Left, Louis Althusser, reacting against Sartrean voluntarism, dissolved the subject by reinterpreting Marxism as a theoretical anti-humanism.[1]

1

The advance of structuralism, far from being deflected or halted by the new reading of Marxism, was accelerated by it. After the events of 1968 Althusser tried to adjust his theory but, on the whole, he did not develop his work. The consequence was the gradual effacement and dissolution of Althusserian Marxism by the mid-seventies.

Post-structuralists, like Foucault, want to deconstruct the conceptions by means of which we have so far understood the human. The term 'subject' helps us to conceive of human reality as a construction, as a product of signifying activities which are both culturally specific and generally unconscious. The category of the subject calls into question the notion of the self synonymous with consciousness; it 'decentres' consciousness.

The post-structuralists, then, also want to dissolve the subject; in a sense it could be said that Derrida and Foucault do not have a 'theory' of the subject. The exception is Lacan, who is committed to the subject because of his Hegelian philosophical formation and his commitment to psychoanalysis. What most of these theorists do not understand is that structure and subject are interdependent categories. The notion of a stable structure really depends on a subject distinct from it. One can see that a wholesale attack on the subject was in due course bound to subvert the notion of structure as well.

Secondly, both structuralism and post-structuralism make a *critique of historicism*. They have an antipathy to the notion that there is an overall pattern in history. A famous example is Lévi-Strauss's criticism of Sartre in *The Savage Mind*, in which he attacks Sartre's view of historical materialism and his assumption that present-day society is superior to past cultures.[2] He then goes on to say that Sartre's historicist view of history is not a valid cognitive enterprise. We will see in later discussions that Foucault writes about history without having the notion of progress, and that Derrida says there is no end point in history.

Thirdly, there is a *critique of meaning*. While philosophy in Britain was heavily influenced by theories of language during the early years of this century (I am thinking of the work of Wittgenstein, Ayer and others), this was not the

case in France. It could be said that, in a way, structuralism
is the delayed entry of language in French philosophy. It
may be remembered that Saussure emphasized the distinction
between the signifier and the signified. The sound image
made by the word 'apple' is the signifier, and the *concept*
of an apple is the signified. The structural relationship
between the signifier and the signified constitutes a linguistic
sign, and language is made up of these. The linguistic sign
is arbitrary; this means that it stands for something by
convention and common usage, not by necessity. Saussure
also stressed the point that each signifier acquired its
semantic value only by virtue of its differential position
within the structure of language.[3] In this conception of the
sign there is a precarious balance between signifier and
signified.

In post-structuralism, broadly speaking, the signified is
demoted and the signifier made dominant. This means there
is no one-to-one correspondence between propositions and
reality. Lacan, for example, writes of 'the incessant sliding
of the signified under the signifier'.[4] The post-structuralist
philosopher Derrida goes further; he believes in a system of
floating signifiers pure and simple, with no determinable
relation to any extra-linguistic referents at all.[5]

Fourthly, there is a *critique of philosophy*. In his early
work Althusser wrote of 'theoretical' practice and argued
that Marxist philosophy was a science.[6] He made a clear
distinction between the young Marx, who wrote within a
Hegelian, ideological problematic, and the older Marx who,
with his understanding of economic concepts and processes,
was a great scientist. It should be noted that when the
structuralists moved language into the centre of French
thought this was done in an anti-philosophical way—an
approach similar to that taken earlier by Comte and
Durkheim.

Having outlined some of the similarities, the continuities,
between structuralism and post-structuralism, I want to
mention some of the characteristic features of post-structuralism. While structuralism sees truth as being 'behind' or
'within' a text, post-structuralism stresses the interaction of
reader and text as a productivity. In other words, reading

has lost its status as a passive consumption of a product to become performance. Post-structuralism is highly critical of the unity of the stable sign (the Saussurean view). The new movement implies a shift from the signified to the signifier: and so there is a perpetual detour on the way to a truth that has lost any status or finality. Post-structuralists have produced critiques of the classical Cartesian conception of the unitary subject—the subject/author as originating consciousness, authority for meaning and truth. It is argued that the human subject does not have a unified consciousness but is structured by language. Post-structuralism, in short, involves a critique of metaphysics, of the concepts of causality, of identity, of the subject, and of truth. All this may seem difficult and abstract at the moment, but these issues will be clarified in the chapters that follow.

There is more continuity between structuralism and post-structuralism than between structuralism and phenomenology. But there are many surprises and contradictions. Lacan, a Freudian psychoanalyst, has studied Hegel. Derrida, a post-structuralist, has studied Husserl and Heidegger deeply. Foucault's historical studies are based on philosophical assumptions drawn from Nietzsche.

The first half of this text is an introduction to the differing theories, the rival programmes, of the leading post-structuralists: Jacques Lacan, Jacques Derrida and Michel Foucault. These thinkers share a characteristic philosophical position which is incompatible with the concept of structure but is also quite radically anti-scientific. They question the status of science itself, and the possibility of the objectivity of any language of description or analysis. They reject the assumptions implicit in the Saussurian model of linguistics on which structuralism was based. The topics explored in Chapters 1, 2 and 3 include: psychoanalysis, the nature and role of language, the self and desire, deconstruction, the rise of instrumental reason, the expansion of apparatuses of social control, and the interconnections between knowledge and power.

In Chapter 4 I examine the work of the 'younger generation' of post-structuralists, such as Gilles Deleuze and Felix Guattari, Jean-François Lyotard, and others (the 'new philosophers'), and argue that many of the characteristic beliefs of post-structuralists have their roots in Nietzsche's thought. Chapter 5 explores Lyotard's thesis about the changing nature of knowledge in computerized societies, of what he calls the 'postmodern condition'. This is followed by a discussion on the current controversy about postmodernism and its critique of the Enlightenment project.

CHAPTER 1

Lacan and psychoanalysis

INTRODUCTION

It could be said that the Marxist dialogue with psychoanalysis began in 1963 when Louis Althusser, the leading communist philosopher in France, invited Jacques Lacan to hold his seminars at the École Normale.[1] During this period there must have been considerable interdisciplinary activity; at any rate, a year later Althusser published the famous article 'Freud and Lacan'.[2] He argued that both Marx and Freud invented new sciences. Each discovered a new object of knowledge. They both defined a new way of knowing about the social, but, not surprisingly, they were weighed down by the cultural baggage of their time. Freud 'thought' his discovery in concepts borrowed from biology, mechanics and the psychology of his day. Marx thought his discovery using Hegelian notions of the subject. It is fascinating to read how Althusser sees Lacan as being involved in a similar project to his own. Just as he, Althusser, is trying to rethink Marxism without any reference to Hegel's absolute subject, he sees Lacan as trying to think psychoanalysis without any reference to a unified conception of self or ego.

A few years later, during the May '68 uprising, it was felt by many students and workers that a liberated politics could only emerge from liberated interpersonal relationships, and there was an explosion of interest in Lacanian psychoanalysis—a movement which seemed to reconcile existentialism and Marxism. A part of existentialism's popular appeal may have been that it provided a way to think through the issues of choice and individual responsibility. But as a theory of the self existentialism remained within Cartesianism. Its psychology tended to portray the individual as a rational, conscious actor who could understand the basis for his action. It remained firmly rooted in a philosophy of individual autonomy and rational choice.

At the time of the May '68 events people were very concerned with questions of self-expression, desire and sexuality, and Lacan's theory offered a way of thinking about the social and the linguistic construction of the self, of thinking through the problem of *the individual and society*. For Lacan there is no separation between self and society. Human beings become social with the appropriation of language; and it is language that constitutes us as a subject. Thus, we should not dichotomize the individual and society. Society inhabits each individual.

It is often said that Lacan wants to be understood only by those who want to make an effort. I think we should make the effort. Lacan's writing, which exemplifies his views about language, is very allusive. His language fuses the theoretical and the poetic. His associative style is intended to slow the reader down. His text is not there to convince, but to do something to you. He relies heavily on punning and word games, and he uses symbols, signs etc. to express himself without referring to ordinary language. He wants to resist the over-simplification of much psychoanalytic writing. He also wants to subvert the normalization that everyday language imposes.

I believe that Lacan's unique achievement was that he fused phenomenology and structuralism. His early work coincided with the growth of French phenomenology and he was influenced by the thought of Hegel and Heidegger. Structuralism offered Lacan a way of talking about *systems* of interpretation. His work is fascinating in that it keeps sliding between phenomenology and structuralism. Phenomenology stresses the free self (the subject); structuralism emphasizes language determinism. Lacan uses structuralism but never rejects the subject.

Lacan also belongs, in part, to the hermeneutic tradition, which states that social phenomena always have meaning and that the task of the social sciences is not to explain (as traditional psychiatry seeks to do) but to understand. Psychoanalysis is a method of interpretation. However, Lacan is aware that in the act of interpretation we often impose our own assumptions.

His doctoral thesis 'On Paranoid Psychosis and its Relation to the Personality' is very interesting because he wrote it before Saussure's work on structuralist linguistics was available.[3] At that time he had not yet become a psychoanalyst; he was still a psychiatrist. What is revealing is the angle from which he approaches Freud and the way in which he repudiates physiological reductionism.

One of the main features of Lacan's work is that it is implacably anti-biological. The accepted view in the 1930s, for example, was that madness had organic causes. Lacan argues that organicist accounts cannot explain madness. Madness is a discourse, an attempt at communication, that must be interpreted. We have to understand rather than give causal explanations. He emphasizes that the personality is not 'the mind' but the whole being. We cannot separate a person's psychology from his or her personal history.

When Lacan became a psychoanalyst he made a few tentative criticisms of Freud. The main one was that Freud made a number of biologistic assumptions. Lacan's view is that biology is always interpreted by the human subject, refracted through language; that there is no such thing as 'the body' before language. It could be said that by shifting all descriptions from a biological-anatomic level to a symbolic one he shows how culture imposes meaning on anatomical parts.

Lacan denigrates not only behaviourist psychologists such as Pavlov and Skinner but also (American) ego psychologists such as Fromm and Horney. The latter stress the adaptation of the individual to the social environment. Lacan argues that they have watered down and sweetened Freud's ideas about the unconscious and infant sexuality.[4] Ego psychology asserts that 'self-improvement' is possible without calling society into question.

Lacan often asserts that he is returning to Freud, but this should not be taken too literally. He retains the main concepts but juggles with them to create a new system of thought. A subtle thinker, he offers us a rigorous reformulation of Freud. He is looking for objectivity, but not the objectivity of natural science. He is very interested in mathematical logic *and* poetry, and in his own writing tries to fuse them. His theory of language is such that he could not return to Freud: texts cannot have an unambiguous, pristine meaning. In his view, analysts must relate directly with the unconscious and this means that they must be practitioners of the language of the unconscious—that of poetry, puns, internal rhymes. In word play causal links dissolve and associations abound.

OVERVIEW

Lacan's psychoanalytic theory is partly based upon the discoveries of structural anthropology and linguistics. One of his main beliefs is that the unconscious is a hidden structure which resembles that of language. Knowledge of the world, of others and of self is determined by language. Language is the precondition for the act of becoming aware of oneself as a distinct entity. It is the I–Thou dialectic, defining the subjects by their mutual opposition, which founds subjectivity. But language is also the vehicle of a social given, a culture, prohibitions and laws. The young child is fashioned and will be indelibly marked by it without being aware of it. Let us look at some of the main stages in Lacan's theory.

In *Beyond the Pleasure Principle* Freud describes a child's game.[5] The child had a cotton reel with a piece of string tied to it. Holding the string he would throw the reel over the edge of his cot and utter sounds that Freud interpreted as being an attempt at the German *'fort'*, meaning 'gone' or 'away'. He would then pull the reel back into his field of vision, greeting its reappearance with a joyful *'da'* ('there'). This game allowed the eighteen-month-old child to bear without protest the painful experience of his mother's absence, to cope with her disappearance and reappearance.

It illustrates the birth of language in its autonomy from reality and allows a better understanding of how language distances us from the lived experience of the Real. The distancing from the lived experience is effected in two stages: the child moves from the mother to the reel and finally to language.

The first articulation of the 'I' occurs in what Lacan calls the mirror stage. Lacan often refers to the mirror stage as it prefigures the whole dialectic between alienation and subjectivity.[6] Self-recognition in the mirror is effected (somewhere between the ages of six and eight months) in three successive stages. At first, the child who is together with an adult in front of a mirror confuses his own reflection with that of his adult companion. In the second phase the child acquires the notion of the image and understands that the reflection is not a real being. Finally, in the third stage, he realizes not only that the reflection is an image, but that the image is his own and is different from the image of the other.

Lacan sees, in a way similar to Lévi-Strauss, the Oedipus complex as the pivot of humanization, as a transition from the natural register of life to a cultural register of group exchange and therefore of laws, language and organization. Lacan contends that at first the child does not merely desire contact with the mother and her care; it wishes, perhaps unconsciously, to be the complement of what is lacking in her: the phallus. At this stage the child is not a subject but a 'lack', a nothing.

In the second stage the father intervenes; he deprives the child of the object of its desire and he deprives the mother of the phallic object. The child encounters the Law of the father. The third stage is that of identification with the father. The father reinstates the phallus as the object of the mother's desire and no longer as the child-complement to what is lacking in her. There is, then, a symbolic castration: the father castrates the child by separating it from its mother. This is the debt which must be paid if one is to become completely one's self.

It needs to be stressed that the Oedipus complex for Lacan is not a stage like any other in genetic psychology: it is the moment in which the child humanizes itself by becoming aware of the self, the world and others. The resolution of the Oedipus complex liberates the subject by giving him, with his Name, a place in the family constellation, an original signifier of self and subjectivity. It promotes him in his realization of self through participation in the world of culture, language and civilization.[7]

As I mentioned earlier, Lacan has rethought Freud in the wider framework provided by linguistics and structural anthropology. In his view the unconscious shows itself in dreams, jokes, slips of the tongue, symptoms. The unconscious is comparable in structure to a language. In fact, Lacan argues that language is the condition for the unconscious, that it creates and gives rise to the unconscious. Like conscious discourse, the formations of the unconscious (dreams etc.) are saying something quite different from what they appear to say. These formations are governed by the same mechanisms as language, namely metaphor and metonymy. At certain privileged points, such as in slips of the tongue and in some jokes, language seems to be torn apart. Conscious discourse is rather like those manuscripts where a first text has been rubbed out and covered by a second. In such manuscripts the first text can be glimpsed through the gaps in the second. The true speech—the unconscious—breaks through usually in a veiled and incomprehensible form.

Lacan suggests that, thanks to human beings' metaphoric ability, words convey multiple meanings and we use them to signify something quite different from their concrete meaning. This possibility of signifying something other than what is being said determines language's autonomy from meaning. Lacan insists on the autonomy of the signifier. He assimilates the metaphoric and metonymic processes of language to condensation and displacement respectively.[8] All the formations of the unconscious use these stylistic devices to outwit censorship.

Throughout his work Lacan strives to denounce the common illusion which identifies the ego with the self. In contrast to those who say 'I think, therefore I am' Lacan asserts: 'I think where I am not, therefore I am where I do not think.'[9] Or, 'I think where I cannot say that I am.'

Having provided a general introduction to Lacan's theory, I will now focus on some important aspects of his work: the relation between self and language; problems of self and identity; the main theoretical differences between Lacan and Freud; the influence on Lacan of Hegel; the meaning of need, demand and desire; the sense of loss.

SELF AND LANGUAGE

Lacan's theory cannot be presented coherently without a discussion of the function of language. He has a complete theory of language, which he links with subjectivity. He believes that there could not be a human subject without language but that the subject cannot be reduced to language. This is a circular (and not a reciprocal) relationship in which language has privilege. Lacan writes (in *The Mirror Stage*) that it is the ability to speak that distinguishes the subject. It is this feature that separates the social from the natural world. *There is no subject independent of language.* Lacan is highly critical of those encounter-therapy groups that tend to deny the role of verbal language and imply that the body and its gestures are more direct.

While Saussure implied that we can somehow stand outside language, Lacan insists that we are all immersed in everyday language and cannot get out of it. There is no such thing as metalanguage. We all have to represent ourselves in language. Indeed our only access to others is through language. (According to Lacan a psychotic person is someone who has not learnt what language is.)[10]

Saussure regarded the relationship between signifiers and signified as stable and predictable. He argued for the possibility of anchoring particular signifiers to particular signifieds in order to form linguistic signs. In Lacan's view, on the other hand, meaning emerges only through discourse, as a consequence of displacements along a signifying chain. Like Derrida, Lacan insists upon the commutability of the signified, upon the capacity of every signified to function in turn as a signifier. A consequences of the non-representational status of language is, of course, that the signified is always provisional.

In a Lacanian view of language a signifier always signifies another signifier; no word is free from metaphoricity (a metaphor is one signifier in the place of another). Lacan talks of *glissement* (slippage, slide) along the signifying chain, from signifier to signifier. Since any signifier can receive signification retrospectively, after the fact, no signification is ever closed, ever satisfied.[11] Each word is only definable in terms of other words. Moreover, each word uttered only makes complete sense when the sentence is finished; and it is perhaps only the very last word uttered which retrospectively establishes the full sense of each word that came before. From anything that is said it cannot be predicted what is going to be said. Any 'sentence' can always be added to. No sentence is ever completely saturated. There is no natural link between signifier and signified. In repression, for example, one signifier comes to substitute for another. The old signifier and what it signifies is 'pushed down' to the unconscious. In the course of a lifetime the individual builds up many chains of signification, always substituting new terms for old and always increasing the distance between the signifier that is accessible and visible and all those that are unconscious.

It is true that at the end of his life Lacan became interested in the possibility of expressing the laws of the unconscious in terms of mathematical statements called 'mathemes'; some people think that this was because he believed that through the process of formalization we might be able to find out what we *cannot* mathematize.

To illustrate that there is no unequivocal meaning, Lacan relates the following story:

A train arrives at a station. A little boy and a little girl, brother and sister, are seated in a compartment face to face next to the window through which the buildings along the station platform can be seen passing as the train pulls to a stop. 'Look', says the brother, 'we're at Ladies!'; 'Idiot!' replies his sister, 'Can't you see we're at Gentlemen'.[12]

In this story each child is able to see only one of the rooms;

each child sees a one-to-one correspondence between the word and the 'thing'—a way of understanding the relationship between signifier and signified that is totally inadequate. Note that it is the girl who sees 'Gentlemen' and the boy who sees 'Ladies', as if one could only see the sex one is not. Through the biological given of sitting on one side of the compartment or the other each sex is placed in a structure and as such is unable to see that structure. Lacan seems to be saying: we are all sitting on one side of the compartment or the other; we are all subject to the blindness imposed by our seats in the compartment; there is no other way of being on the train(chain).[13]

SELF AND IDENTITY

It should be stressed that Lacan uses the idea of a child before the mirror as a metaphor. The notion of reflection is a common one (especially in German Idealist philosophy), stemming from Hegel. In this philosophy there is a concern with questions such as: What is it to be conscious of oneself? How do we recognize the self? What is that 'something' that reflects consciousness back onto itself? In self-consciousness the subject and the object are identical; but can I reflect on the self and reflect on that reflection? Can the self that is self of consciousness grasp the self of consciousness? When we see ourselves we see only a look. We do not get nearer to what we are. This is called 'the infinity of reflection'.[14]

Another important Lacanian idea is 'the dialectic of recognition'. This refers to the idea that we get knowledge of what we are from how others respond to us. It is useful to compare D. W. Winnicott's discussion of the mirror role with Lacan's view. Winnicott suggests that the first mirror is the mother's face.[15] He argues that other people provide the stability of our self-identity. Some feminists have criticized him because he unquestioningly focuses only on the 'mother' role. (Moreover, what happens if the mother is ill or mentally disturbed and cannot send back an image?)

In contrast with Winnicott, Lacan says that we are never

going to get a stable image. We try to interpret our relation to others but there is always the possibility of misinterpretation. There is always a gap, a misrecognition. We can never be certain of the meaning of the other's response. We have an idea of our identity but it does not correspond with reality: the mirror image is back to front.

Our notion of the self as an isolated self is in some way connected with bourgeois individualism. (Lacan hints, however, that it may always be like this.) Lacan continually attacks the American psychologists (Erich Fromm and Karen Horney again) who keep stressing the ego. In his view the stable ego is illusory. We can shed the illusions of the ego only asymptotically (in geometry an asymptote is a curve approaching a straight line but never reaching it short of infinity).[16]

Lacan insists that we do not have a fixed set of characteristics. This is very much the view Sartre expressed in *Being and Nothingness*.[17] In Sartre's theory consciousness can never grasp itself. Reflection always turns the subject into an object. Sartre rejects the idea that drives determine consciousness. He suggests that as soon as we say, 'I'm like that—that's me', we have made ourselves into an object. We often build up a set of characteristics retrospectively. Sartre insists that we are more than a fixed set of categories. We should not think of ourselves as merely a set of characterizations. Nor should we go to the other extreme and conceive of ourselves as pure nothingness.

Lacan argues that we are never any one of our attributes. There is no truth if by truth is meant that an individual expresses an inherent characteristic. Sceptical of any 'underlying truth', he writes: 'If Freud had brought to man's knowledge nothing more than the truth that there is such a thing as the true, there would be no Freudian discovery. Freud would belong to a line of moralists . . . .'[18]

Lacan stresses the point that there is no subject except in representation, but that no representation captures us completely. I can neither be totally defined nor can I escape all definition. I am the quest for myself. Lacan believes that how we present ourselves is always subject to interpretation by others. On the other hand, any attempt to 'totalize' someone else, to grasp the other completely, is bound to fall short—no description does the other justice. Moreover, one can only see onself as one *thinks* others see one. There is an inherent tension, a feeling of threat, because one's identity depends on recognition by the other. This is the theme of Hegel's story of Master and Slave. I will give a detailed exposition of it later in the chapter. For the moment it is only necessary to say that Hegel argued that consciousness cannot grasp itself without recognition by others. The Master demands recognition from the Slave but this is a self-defeating process. He feels threatened because recognition of himself depends exclusively on the Slave. To generalize from the story, we would like to reduce others to an instrument—a mirror. There is a moment of aggression when we want to overcome our dependency. (We often hear people say: 'I've got to insist on my independence.')

But is there a possibility of mutual recognition? Lacan suggests that intersubjectivity can never be fully attained because we can never enter another person's consciousness completely. Full mutual recognition is not possible partly because of the ambiguity of signifiers. There is a gulf between saying and meaning. All this is reminiscent of Sartre, who says that when we love another we want that person's love—and this attitude instrumentalizes love. As soon as one person is the subject, the other is the object. Lacan belongs to the tradition that believes that the subject and the object are irreconcilably divided. Undoubtedly he has an ontology: we all have a need for wholeness, a longing for the state of unity, but the achievement of plenitude is a logical impossibility.

FREUD AND LACAN

There are many differences between Freud and Lacan and in this section I will discuss some of them. I will focus particularly on their different conceptualizations of the ego, the unconscious, the dream, and the Oedipus complex.

In Freud's early work the ego is connected with the reality

principle, and the unconscious is related to the pleasure principle. Later Freud reformulated his theory: the ego is formed through an identification with parental figures. The important point to note is that Freud never says the ego is illusory.

Lacan's argument is the opposite of this. He believes that identification stabilizes the individual but at the same time takes us away from ourselves. He says that Freud starts from individuals' drives and their satisfactions and that he neglects social dimensions. For Lacan, however, the subject-to-subject relation, what we call intersubjectivity, is there right from the beginning.

Freud believed that the aim of analysis was to integrate a drive into 'the harmony of the ego'. Lacan, of course, would never use such a phrase. While for Freud the unconscious has a threatening aspect, in Lacan it is the locus of 'truth', of authenticity. And yet Lacan believes that the unconscious cannot be an object of knowledge; the ego projects itself and then fails to recognize itself. Self-knowledge, the notion that the self can reflect on itself, is not possible.

While Freud seems to have believed in the unconscious as a substantive concept, for Lacan 'the unconscious is not the real place of another discourse'. Lacan proclaims that the unconscious is neither primordial nor instinctual. The unconscious is implicit in everything we say and do. However, in trying to grasp the unconscious we lose it—like 'twice-lost Eurydice'. The unconscious is that which we can never know, but this does not mean that the effort is not worth while.

Two processes are of central importance in Freudian theory: the primary process, which is associated with the unconscious (irrational thought), and the secondary process, which is associated with the conscious (logical thought).[19] When the object of satisfaction is denied and life is difficult we often retreat from reality and overcome frustration by hallucinating. But after a certain time, in order for us to survive, the reality principle comes into play. The ego intervenes, separates things out and puts a stop to the hallucination. This secondary process is continually being interrupted by the unconscious. Human rationality is a thin, fragile 'façade' which the unconscious keeps bursting asunder. Again, Lacan rejects Freud's view. For him the unconscious is neither primordial nor instinctual; the secondary process is more like the primary process than Freud thought.

It is in the dream that we can see the operation of the primary process. As Freud said, it is the dream that is 'the royal road to the unconscious'. For Lacan a dream is not a pictorial representation; though it happens to be an image *a dream is really a text*:

> The dream is like the parlour-game in which one is supposed to get the spectators to guess some well-known saying or variant of it solely by dumb show. That the dream uses speech makes no difference since for the unconscious it is only one among several elements of the representation. It is precisely the fact that both the game and the dream run up against a lack of taxematic material for the representation of such logical articulations as causality, contradiction, hypothesis, etc. that proves they are a form of writing rather than of mime.[20]

It is in dreams that the processes of condensation and displacement take place. According to Lacan, in condensation there is a superimposition of the signifiers which metaphor takes as its field. A simple image can thus have different meanings. Displacement, another means used by the unconscious to foil censorship, is associated with metonymy.

Though Lacan believes that the desire of the dream is to communicate, he does not ever say to an analysand 'this is what you really want', or 'this is what your dream really means'. If he did, this would be another alienation. In his view the subject is a process and cannot be defined.

Freud was very interested in the relationship between nature and culture and emphasized the dominance of culture over nature. Lacan rejects the notion of an innate human nature. Nature, for Lacan, is the Real which is out there but impossible to grasp in a pure state because it is always mediated through language. In Freud's work one is aware of a tragic element in the nature–culture dichotomy. In Lacan, tragedy lies in the fact that we have a perpetual lack of wholeness.

Freud and Lacan also have different views of the Oedipus

complex. In Freud's theory the Oedipus complex must be understood in the context of his theory of psychosexuality. In the first stage of infant sexuality, the oral stage, there are fantasies of incorporating and devouring. The second stage, the anal/sadistic, is associated with submission and domination. In the third, the phallic stage, the boy wants the mother exclusively. He is threatened with castration and develops an impotence fear. There is an introjection of the father's threat which leads, finally, to a resolution of the complex.

Lacan tries to rationalize Freud's thesis by not taking the Oedipus complex literally. Whereas Freud's Oedipal Father might be taken for a real, biological father, Lacan's Name-of-the-Father operates in the register of language. The Name-of-the-Father is the Law. The legal assignation of a father's name to a child is meant to call a halt to uncertainty about the identity of the father.

Lacan does not abandon the idea of the focus on the oral, the anal and the phallic, but he says that these stages are intersubjective. Freud's theory refers to the physical and not the symbolic. In Freud the penis is a guarantee of a possible union with the mother. Lacan transforms all this to the level of the symbolic. This is why he writes not of the penis but of the phallus.[21]

Lacanians, separating the two notions 'penis' and 'phallus', argue that there is no phallus inequity; that is, neither sex can be or have the phallus. The penis is what men have and women do not, the phallus is the attribute of power which neither men nor women have. Lacan suggests that all our fantasies are symbolic representations of the desire for wholeness. We tend to think that if we were the phallus or had the other's phallus we would then, somehow, be whole. In other words, the phallus is the signifier of an original desire for a perfect union with the Other. The phallus refers to plenitude; it is the signifier of the wholeness that we lack.

There is another difference between Freud and Lacan. The former held that rational discourse was possible, even though it was often distorted by unconscious forces. For Lacan discourse *constitutes* the unconscious. Language and desire are related. In Lacan desire is ontological, a struggle for wholeness rather than a sexual force. 'Desire is the metonymy of the desire to want to be.'

While Freud talks of instincts and drives Lacan talks of desire—a concept which comes from Kojève's lectures on Hegel. These lectures are important, as Lacan, Sartre and others were highly influenced by them. Kojève describes the development of self-consciousness. Hegel insists that self-consciousness develops out of the biological self. Self-consciousness would not be possible without an organic lack. A lack ('I feel hungry') makes us aware of ourselves as a being that needs something. Hegel continues that for a desire to develop in us we need to focus on a specific object. When we desire not a thing but another's desire we become human. Moreover, desire is mobile, not static; a desire can be continually negated, but it continues.

HEGEL AND LACAN

As what Lacan means by desire is drawn from Hegel, I want to retell in this section Hegel's metaphoric story of the Master and the Slave before I try to elucidate the Lacanian concepts of need, demand and desire.[22] What follows may seem a digression, but this 'detour' through Hegel is necessary because the Master/Slave theme, in both Marxist and Nietzschean versions, constantly reappears in contemporary social thought.

Hegel remarks that we all know that the person who attentively contemplates a thing is 'absorbed' by this thing and forgets himself. He may perhaps talk about the thing but he will never talk about himself; in his discourse the word 'I' will not occur.

For this word to appear, something other than purely passive contemplation must be present. And this other thing is, according to Hegel, Desire. Indeed, when man experiences a desire, when he is hungry, for example, and becomes aware of it he necessarily becomes aware of himself. Desire is always revealed to the individual as *his* desire, and to express desire he must use the word 'I'.[23]

Desire dis-quiets him and moves him to action. Action tends to satisfy desire but can do so only by the 'negation', the destruction or at least the transformation of the desired object: to satisfy hunger, for example, the food must be destroyed or in any case transformed. Thus, all action is 'negating'. The being that eats creates and preserves its own reality by overcoming a reality other than its own, by the 'transformation' of an alien reality into its own reality, by the 'assimilation', the 'internalization', of an 'external' reality. Generally speaking, the 'I' of Desire is an emptiness that receives a real positive content by a negating action that satisfies Desire in destroying, transforming and assimilating the desired non-I.

Desire, being the revelation of an emptiness, the presence of an absence, is something essentially different from the desired thing. Desire is directed towards another Desire, another greedy emptiness, another 'I'. Desire is human only if one desires not the body but the Desire of the other; that is to say, if one wants to be 'desired' or, rather, 'recognized' in one's human value. All Desire is desire for a value. To desire the Desire of another is really to desire 'recognition'.

MASTER AND SLAVE

If there is a multiplicity of desires seeking universal recognition, it is obvious that the action that is born of these desires can—at least in the beginning—be nothing but a life-and-death fight. It is assumed that the fight ends in such a way that both adversaries remain alive. Now, if this is to occur, one must suppose that one of the adversaries, preferring to live rather than die, gives in to the other and submits to him, recognizing him as the Master without being recognized by him. The Master, unable to recognize the other who recognizes him, finds himself in an impasse.

The Master makes the Slave work in order to satisfy his own desires. To satisfy the desires of the Master, the Slave has to repress his own instincts (for example, in the preparation of food that he will not eat), to negate or 'overcome' himself.[24] The Slave transcends himself by working, that is, he educates himself. In his work he transforms things and transforms himself at the same time. In becoming master of Nature by work, the Slave frees himself from Nature, from his own nature, and from the Master. It is because work is an auto-creative act that it can raise him from slavery to freedom. The future and history hence belong not to the warlike Master, who either dies or preserves himself indefinitely in 'identity to himself', but to the working Slave.

To summarize, according to Hegel it is a fight to the death for the sake of recognition that leads to a relation between a free man and a man who is enslaved to him. Hence man is necessarily either Master or Slave. But the difference between Master and Slave can be overcome in the course of time. Mastery and Slavery, then, are not given or innate characteristics. Man is not born slave or free but creates himself as one or the other through free or voluntary action. In short, the character of the Master/Slave opposition is the motive principle of the historical process. All of history is nothing but the progressive negation of Slavery by the Slave. Finally, the thesis of Mastery and the antithesis of Slavery are dialectically 'overcome'.

IDENTITY AND NEGATIVITY

Thanks to identity every being remains the same being, eternally identical to itself and different from the others. But thanks to negativity an identical being can negate or overcome its identity with itself and become other than it is, even its own opposite. Identity and negativity do not exist in an isolated state. Just like totality itself they are only complementary aspects of one and the same real being.[25]

The thesis describes the given material to which the action is going to be applied, the antithesis reveals this action itself as well as the thought which animates it ('the project'), while the synthesis shows the result of that action, that is, the completed and objectively real product. The new product is also given and can provoke other negating actions. Human beings are always negating the given. Negativity is the negation of identity. Human beings are truly free or really human only in and by effective negation of the given real. Negativity, then, is nothing other than human freedom. The freedom which is realized and manifested as dialectical or negating action is thereby essentially a creation. What is involved is not replacing one given by another given, but overcoming the given in favour of what does not (yet) exist. In short, man is neither identity nor negativity alone but totality or synthesis; that is, he 'overcomes' himself while preserving and sublimating himself.

In my view this discussion has a direct bearing on education. All education implies a long series of auto-negations effected by the child. As Kojève remarks, '. . . it is only because of these auto-negations ('repressions') that every "educated" child is not only a trained animal (which is 'identical' to itself and in itself) but a truly human or "complex" being; although in most cases, he is human only to a very small extent, since "education" (that is, auto-negations) generally stops too soon.'[26]

PARTICULARLITY AND UNIVERSALITY

Particularity refers to the individual agent. Every man, to the extent that he is human, would like—on the one hand—to be different from all others. But on the other hand he would like to be recognized, in his unique particularity itself, as a positive value; and he would like this recognition to be shown as many people as possible. Universality refers to the social aspect of man's existence. It is only in and by the universal recognition of human particularity that individuality realizes and manifests itself.

Individuality is a synthesis of the particular and the universal, the universal being the negation or the antithesis of the particular, which is the thetical given, identical to itself. In other words, individuality is a totality and the

being which is individual is, by the very fact, dialectical.
Man is and exists only to the extent that he overcomes
himself dialectically (i.e. while preserving and sublimating
himself). The opposition of particularity and universality is
fundamental for Hegel. In his view history will develop by
the formation of a society, of a state, in which the strictly
particular, personal, individual value of each is recognized
as such, in its very particularity, by all. The synthesis of
particularity and universality is possible only after the
'overcoming' of the opposition between the Master and the
Slave, since the synthesis of the particular and the universal
is also the synthesis of Mastery and Slavery.[27]

THE DESIRE FOR DESIRE

What use does Lacan make of these Hegelian insights? We
all have physical needs to satisfy. The child in the oral
phase, for example, wants the mother's breast. It makes an
appeal to its mother to have its needs met. This is the
transformation from need to demand, but there is also the
desire for love, for recognition. Needs, then, are biological.
In demand the biological is mediated; a demand is always
specific. Desire is what cannot be specified by demand.[28] A
child cries. The mother gives a bar of chocolate; but the
child can never know whether this action was performed
for the satisfaction of its need or as an act of love. Lacan
believes that such a response is inherently ambiguous. And
because the response is ambiguous the demand is repeated,
repeated . . . *ad infinitum*.

Need, demand, desire—how are these three categories
interconnected? A child cries. It can use physical hunger as
a vehicle for a communication. Sometimes the food satisfies
a physical need but it can also become symbolically freighted.
There can be a split between need and desire. In an account
of anorexia Lacan states how a young woman is given food
but wants love. The meaning of demand is not intrinsic but
is partly determined by the response by the other to the
demand. Though our demand is specific we can never be

certain of other people's responses to ourselves. After all, how do you give love?

People can continually be making a demand but they need not be conscious of it. A demand is the means of revealing desire, but it is oblique. Desire is desire for the Other but it has to be interpreted. Lacan says that need is cancelled by demand which re-emerges on the other side of desire. We often want an object that could be given only to *us*, but there is no such object. A demand is for a response, but that response is never particular enough. We can never be certain that others love us for our unique particularity.

It could be said that some people are too confident that they are loved. Lacan suggests that their identities may become rather rigid. And there are other people who lack confidence. Desire emerges when satisfaction of need is not enough, when there is a doubt or gap which cannot be closed. Desire arises out of the lack of satisfaction and it pushes you to another demand. In other words, it is the disappointment of demand that is the basis of the growth of desire.

THE SENSE OF LOSS

In this section I will retell Lacan's story and will focus specifically on the sense of loss or lack that the subject undergoes. You will have noticed that Lacan's theory of the subject reads like a classic narrative; it begins with birth and then moves in turn through the territorialization of the body, the mirror stage, access to language and the Oedipus complex. Each of the stages of this narrative is conceived in terms of some kind of self-loss or lack.

Lacan situates the first loss in the history of the subject at the moment of birth. To be more precise, he dates it from the moment of sexual differentiation within the womb; but it is not realized until the separation of the child from the mother at birth. This lack is sexual in definition and has to do with the impossibility of being physiologically both male and female. The notion of an original androgynous whole is central to Lacan's argument. The subject is defined as lacking because it is believed to be a fragment of something larger and primordial.

Let me clarify this briefly. Lacan often makes references to a fable on the subject of love in Plato's *Symposium*.[29] Aristophanes speaks of beings that, 'once upon a time', were globular in shape, with rounded back and sides, four arms and legs and two faces. Strong, energetic and arrogant, they tried to scale the heights of heaven and set upon the gods. Zeus retaliated by cutting them all in half so that each one would be only half as strong.

Now, when the work of bisection was complete it left each half with a desperate yearning for the other and they ran together and flung their arms around each others' necks and asked for nothing better than to be rolled into one. So much so that they began to die. Zeus felt so sorry for them that he devised another scheme. He moved their genitals round to the front and made them propagate among themselves. So you see how far back we can trace our innate love for one another, and how this love is always trying to reintegrate our former nature, to make two into one and to bridge the gulf between one human being and another.

The second loss suffered by the subject occurs after birth but prior to the acquisition of language. The loss in question is inflicted by what might be called the 'pre-Oedipal territorialization' of the subject's body. For a time after its birth the child does not differentiate between itself and the mother upon whose nurture it relies. Then the child's body undergoes a process of differentiation; erotogenic zones are inscribed and the libido is encouraged to follow certain established routes. By indicating the channels through which that libido can move the mother or nurse assists in the conversion of incoherent energy into coherent drives which can later be culturally regulated. The drives possess a coherence which needs do not have, because they are attached to particular corporal zones. As a result of this attachment the drives provide only an indirect expression of the original libidinal flow. Thus very early in its history the subject loses unmediated contact with its own libidinal flows and succumbs to the domination of its culture's genital economy.

'Imaginary' is the term used by Lacan to designate that order of the subject's experience which is dominated by identification and duality. Within the Lacanian scheme it not only precedes the symbolic order, which introduces the subject to language and Oedipal triangulation, but continues to coexist with it afterwards. The imaginary order is best exemplified by the mirror stage.

Lacan tells us that somewhere between the ages of six and eighteen months the subject arrives at an apprehension of both its self and the Other—indeed of itself as Other. This discovery is assisted by the child seeing, for the first time, its own reflection in a mirror. That reflection has a coherence which the subject itself lacks. But this self-recognition is, Lacan insists, a mis-recognition. The mirror stage is a moment of alienation, since to know oneself through an external image is to be defined through self-alienation. The subject, then, has a profoundly ambivalent relationship to that reflection. It loves the coherent identity which the mirror provides. However, because the image remains external to it, it also hates that image. The subject experiences many radical oscillations between contrary emotions.

Lacan believes that once the subject has entered the symbolic order (language) its organic needs pass through the 'defiles' or narrow network of signification and are transformed in a way which makes them thereafter impossible to satisfy. The drives offer only a partial and indirect expression of those needs, but language severs the relationship altogether.

The *fort/da* game can be seen as the child's first signifying chain and hence its entry into language. It should be noted that whereas Freud describes the child's actions in the *fort/da* game as an attempt to diminish the unpleasure caused by his mother's absences, Lacan stresses instead the self-alienation which those actions dramatize. Lacan identifies the toy reel with which the child plays as an *objet petit autre*—that thing the loss of which has resulted in a sense of deficiency or lack. The breast, for example, certainly represents that part of himself that the individual loses at birth and which may serve to symbolize the most profound lost object. (Other objects which enjoy the same privileged status as the breast include the gaze and voice of the mother.) Lacan thus interprets the story as being more about the disappearance of the self than that of the mother. Like Freud Lacan reads the *fort/da* episode as an allegory about the linguistic mastery of the drives. Lacan describes this complete rupture with the drives as the 'fading' of the subject's being, as 'aphanisis'. Not only is the subject thereby split off or partitioned from its own drives, but it is subordinated to a symbolic order which will henceforth determine its identity and desires.

The formation of the unconscious, the emergence of the subject into the symbolic order and the inauguration of desire are all closely connected events. Desire is directed towards ideal representations which remain forever beyond the subject's reach. Since others will be loved only if they are believed to be capable of completing the subject, desire must be understood as fundamentally narcissistic. Object love is nothing more than the continued search for the lost complement.

Lacan conceptualizes the Oedipus complex as a linguistic transaction. He supports this claim by pointing out that the incest taboo can only be articulated through the differentiation of certain cultural members from others by means of linguistic categories like 'father' and 'mother'. Lacan defines the paternal signifier, what he calls the 'Name-of-the-Father', as the all-important one both in the history of the subject and the organization of the larger symbolic field.

This means that Lacan gives us a very different account of sexual difference from that provided by Freud, one in which the privileged term is no longer 'penis' but 'phallus'. The word 'phallus' is used by Lacan to refer to all of those values which are opposed to lack. He is at pains to emphasize its discursive (rather than its anatomical) status, but it seems to have two radically different meanings. On the one hand, the phallus is a signifier for those things which have been partitioned off from the subject during the various stages of its constitution and which will never be restored to it. The phallus is a signifier for the organic reality or needs which the subject relinquishes in order to achieve meaning, in order to gain access to the symbolic register. It signifies that thing whose loss inaugurates desire. On the other hand, the phallus is a signifier for the cultural privileges and positive values which define male subjectivity within patriarchal society but from which the female subject remains isolated. The phallus, in other words, is a signifier both for those things which are lost during the male subject's entry into culture and for those things which are gained.

Lacan believes that the discourse within which the subject finds its identity is always the discourse of the Other—of a symbolic order which transcends the subject and which orchestrates its entire history. An important part is played by sexual difference within that order, and this has made us aware of the phallocentricity of our current practices.

One Lacanian tenet is that subjectivity is entirely relational; it only comes into play through the principle of difference, by the opposition of the 'other' or the 'you' to the 'I'. In other words, subjectivity is not an essence but a set of relationships. It can only be induced by the activation of a signifying system which exists before the individual and which determines his or her cultural identity. Discourse, then, is the agency whereby the subject is produced and the existing order sustained.

CONCLUSION

I will now try to bring some of the threads together by briefly stating what Lacan means by the Imaginary, the Symbolic and the Real. This will also enable me to recapitulate some of the key points of this chapter. It is clear that the Imaginary—a kind of pre-verbal register whose logic is essentially visual—precedes the symbolic as a stage in the development of the psyche. Its moment of formation has been named the 'mirror stage'. At this stage there does not yet exist that ego formation which would permit a child to distinguish its own form from that of others. The child who hits says it has been hit, the child who sees another child fall begins to cry. (It is from Melanie Klein's pioneering psychoanalysis of children that the basic features of the Lecanian Imaginary are drawn.) *The Imaginary order* is pre-Oedipal. The self yearns to fuse with what is perceived as Other. The child confuses others with its own mirror reflections; and since the self is formed from a composite of introjections based on such misrecognitions, it can hardly constitute a unified personality. In other words, we experience a profoundly divided self.

Lacan suggests that the infant's first desire for the mother signifies the wish to be what the mother desires. (*Désir de la mère* refers to the desire for the mother *and* to the mother's desire.) The infant wants to complete the mother, to be what she lacks – the phallus. The child's relationship with the mother is fusional, dual and immediate. Later, the child's desire to be its mother's desire gives way to an identification with the father.

The child's asocial, dual and fusional relationship with its mother is forsworn for the world of symbolic discourse. The father becomes the third term and we enter the symbolic order by accepting his name and interdictions. In the symbolic there is no longer a one-to-one correspondence between things and what they are called—a symbol evokes an open-ended system of meaning. Symbolic signification is social, not narcissistic. It is the Oedipal crisis which marks the child's entrance into the world of the symbolic. The laws of language and society come to dwell within the child as he accepts the father's name and the father's 'no'.

I said earlier that Lacan understands the Oedipus story in terms of language, not in terms of the body, and that there is no such thing as the body before language. Biology is always interpreted by the human subject. But not only biology, all experience is symbolically mediated and has to be interpreted (in the context of social convention).

The Lacanian notion of *the Symbolic order* is an attempt to create mediations between libidinal analysis and the linguistic categories, to provide, in other words, a transcoding scheme which allows us to speak of both within a common conceptual framework. The Oedipus complex is transliterated by Lacan into a linguistic phenomenon which he designates as the discovery by the subject of the Name-of-the-Father. Lacan feels that the apprenticeship of language is an alienation for the psyche but he realizes that it is impossible to return to an archaic, pre-verbal stage of the psyche itself.

I have underlined the point that Lacan places great emphasis on the linguistic development of the child. He argues that the acquisition of a name results in a thoroughgoing transformation of the position of the subject in his object world. There is a determination of the subject by language. The Freudian unconscious is seen in terms of language: 'The unconscious is the discourse of the Other'—a notion that tends to surprise those who associate language with thinking and consciousness.

Lacan's theory has attracted a good deal of interest among feminists because the emphasis on the production of gendered subjectivity via signification (the processes whereby meaning is produced at the same time as subjects are fabricated and positioned in social relations) implies that it is possible to escape the subordination of women inherent in Freud's recourse to biological difference. However, it could be argued that, in privileging the phallus as the sign of difference as opposed to the penis, Lacan's analysis is not any less deterministic than Freud's.[30] This is because Lacan relies heavily on Lévi-Strauss's structural analysis of the incest taboo which, it is said, underlies all human societies. The use of Lévi-Strauss's thesis means that the terms of the debate are fixed around the 'Law of the Father'. Because Lévi-Strauss's theory is a universalist one Lacan's account tends to collapse into an account of a universal subject who is not situated historically.

The third order is the Real. The reality which we can never know is the Real—it lies beyond language ... the reality we must assume although we can never know it. This is the most problematic of the three orders or registers since it can never be experienced immediately, but only by way of the mediation of the other two: 'the Real, or what is

perceived as such, is what resists symbolization absolutely.'
Fredric Jameson, however, thinks that it is not terribly
difficult to say what is meant by the Real in Lacan: 'It is
simply History itself.'[31]

To conclude the chapter, let me now turn to some
criticisms of Lacan. It is often said that he intellectualizes
everything and does not consider the emotions. He is highly
critical, for example, of the Reichian approach which asserts
that we can get to the emotions directly.[32] For Lacan an
emotion is a signifier; it means something but what it means
is an open question. Secondly, as his writings lack clinical
material it is difficult to learn from his procedures or to test
their validity. He seems to be more interested in developing
theory in the university than in clinical practice. (On the
other hand, it could be argued that though Lacan fails to
provide case studies one way out of the problem is to
examine the work of his followers, for example child
psychologists such as Françoise Dolto and Maud Mannoni.)
As he believes that in analysis nothing should be routine or
predictable his sessions are sometimes only ten minutes long!
He argues that psychoanalysis is not a psychology. If it was
a psychology it would be like ethology (the study of animal
behaviour); but the salient difference is that we cannot
predict human behaviour. Moreover, Lacan holds that only
an analyst can authorize himself or herself as an analyst.
But, surely, self-authorization leads to problems about
standards? Is it enough to be told that becoming an analyst
is like becoming a poet, one who has a new, intimate
relationship with language?

There is also a feminist critique of Lacan. Some writers
have argued that his work reinforces Freud's phallocentrism,
albeit at the level of language and not that of anatomy.
Luce Irigaray, a fierce critic of Lacan, asks if the Freudian
reliance on the phallus as a symbolic law is not the result
of patriarchal culture rather than an inherent necessity of
language or biology.[33] She questions why the phallus alone
is guarantor of meaning, why there cannot be 'vagina envy'.
And is Lacan's phallocentric law (that the phallus alone can
represent the symbolic) really the universal law of mankind
or is this the law merely of men? It is clear that in Lacanian

theory certain symbols are privileged over others: the phallus, the Name-of-the-Father, the Law. There does not seem to be any convincing reason, however, why these signifiers in particular should play such a large role in defining and organizing the human psyche. The point of these feminist criticisms is not to deny the reality and current force of the law of the phallus; it is to question its universal and inevitable theoretical status and power.

And then there is also the question of Lacan's philosophical idealism. He proclaims, 'It is the world of words which creates the world of things.' This axiom is fundamental to his thought, since it gives primacy to language over social structure. While language certainly has a determining as well as mediating role in the formation of consciousness of the world, the social system, I would argue, also determines and limits linguistic possibility.

I often wonder whether the study of the Lacanian model of the subject can help us conceive of a different signification, a different subjectivity, and a different symbolic and social order. We certainly need a model that overcomes the opposition between individual and social phenomena.[34] It seems to me vital that some sort of integration be made between Lacanian psychoanalysis and Marxism. This is crucial because no political revolution can be completed until the very character structures inherited from the older, prerevolutionary society, reinforced by its instinctual taboos, have been utterly transformed.[35]

CHAPTER 2

Derrida and deconstruction

INTRODUCTION

Deconstruction, which has attained widespread recognition as one of the most important avant-garde intellectual movements in France and America, is essentially post-phenomenological and post-structuralist. In the history of contemporary deconstruction the leading figure is Jacques Derrida, who published three influential books in 1967: *Of Grammatology, Speech and Phenomena* and *Writing and Difference*.[1] Amongst other things these texts contain powerful critiques of phenomenology (Husserl), linguistics (Saussure), Lacanian psychoanalysis, and structuralism (Lévi-Strauss).

In this chapter I give an exposition of Derrida's thought. Beginning with an outline of his view of language I give an explanation of what he means by phonocentrism and logocentrism. I then present his arguments against the work of Jean-Jacques Rousseau, Claude Lévi-Strauss and Jacques Lacan. There are also sections on his 'predecessors' Freud and Nietzsche and an account of how they have influenced Derrida's thinking on reading texts and the nature of metaphor. After that I examine some metaphors in common use. Finally, after situating metaphor in the context of political and ideological struggle, I discuss the relationship between deconstruction and Marxism.

THE INSTABILITY OF LANGUAGE

In trying to understand Derrida's work one of the most important concepts to grasp is the idea of '*sous rature*', a term usually translated as 'under erasure'. To put a term '*sous rature*' is to write a word, cross it out, and then print both word and deletion. The idea is this: since the word is inaccurate, or rather, inadequate, it is crossed out. Since it is necessary it remains legible. This strategically important device which Derrida uses derives from Martin Heidegger, who often crossed out the word Being (like this: B̶e̶i̶n̶g̶) and let both deletion and word stand because the word was *inadequate yet necessary*. Heidegger felt that Being cannot be contained by, is always prior to, indeed transcends, signification. Being is the final signified to which all signifiers refer, the 'transcendental signified'.

In Derrida's view of language the signifier does not yield us up a signified directly, as a mirror yields up an image. There is no harmonious one-to-one set of correspondences between the level of the signifieds in language. Signifiers and signified are continually breaking apart and reattaching in new combinations, thus revealing the inadequacy of Saussure's model of the sign, according to which the signifier and signified relate as if they were two sides of the same sheet of paper. Indeed, there is no fixed distinction between signifiers and signified. Suppose you want to know the meaning of a signifier, you can look it up in the dictionary; but all you will find will be yet more signifiers, whose signifieds you can in turn look up, and so on. The process is not only infinite but somehow circular: signifiers keep transforming into signifieds, and vice versa, and you never arrive at a final signified which is not a signifier in itself.

In other words, Derrida argues that meaning is not immediately present in a sign. Since the meaning of a sign is a matter of what the sign is *not*, this meaning is always in some sense absent from it too. Meaning is scattered or dispersed along the whole chain of signifiers; it cannot be easily nailed down, it is never fully present in any one sign alone, but is rather a kind of constant flickering of presence and absence together. Reading a text is more like tracing this process of constant flickering than like counting the beads on a necklace.

Now, for Derrida the structure of the sign is determined by the trace (the French meaning carries strong implications of track, footprint, imprint) of that other which is forever absent. This other is, of course, never to be found in its full being. Rather like the answer to a child's question or a definition in a dictionary, one sign leads to another and so on indefinitely . . . .

What is the implication of this? That the projected 'end' of knowledge could ever coincide with its 'means' is an impossible dream of plenitude. No one can make the 'means' (the sign) and the 'end' (meaning) become identical. Sign will always lead to sign, one substituting the other as signifier and signified in turn. For Derrida the sign cannot be taken as a homogeneous unit bridging an origin (referent) and an end (meaning), as semiology, the study of signs, would have it. The sign must be studied 'under erasure', always already inhabited by the trace of another sign which never appears as such.

There is also the fact that language is a temporal process. When I read a sentence the meaning of it is always somehow suspended, something deferred. One signifier relays me to another; earlier meanings are modified by later ones. In each sign there are traces of other words which that sign has excluded in order to be itself. And words contain the trace of the ones which have gone before. Each sign in the chain of meaning is somehow scored over or traced through with all the others, to form a complex tissue which is never exhaustible.

Meaning is never identical with itself; because a sign appears in different contexts it is never absolutely the same. Meaning will never stay quite the same from context to context; the signified will be altered by the various chains of signifiers in which it is entangled.

The implication of this is that language is a much less stable affair than was thought by structuralists such as Lévi-Strauss. None of the elements is absolutely definable; everything is caught up and traced through by everything else. Nothing is ever fully present in signs. It is an illusion for me to believe that I can ever be fully present to you in what I say or write, because to use signs at all entails my meaning being always somehow dispersed, divided and never quite at one with itself. Not only my meaning, indeed, but I myself: since language is something I am made out of, rather than a convenient tool I use, the whole idea that I am a stable, unified entity must also be a fiction.[2]

PHONOCENTRISM–LOGOCENTRISM

Derrida is mainly concerned with the role and function of language and is famous for having developed a procedure called deconstruction. This is a method of reading a text so closely that the author's conceptual distinctions on which the text relies are shown to fail on account of the inconsistent and paradoxical use made of these very concepts within the text as a whole. In other words, the text is seen to fail by its own criteria; the standards or definitions which the text sets up are used reflexively to unsettle and shatter the original distinctions. Derrida has used this technique against Husserl, Rousseau, Saussure, Plato, Freud and others; but the method can be applied to any text.

The method of deconstruction is connected with what Derrida calls the 'metaphysics of presence'. It is Derrida's contention that Husserl, along with almost all other philosophers, relies on the assumption of an immediately available area of certainty. The origin and foundation of most philosophers' theories is presence. In Husserl's case the search for the form of pure expression is at the same time a search for that which is immediately present; thus implicitly, by being present in an unmediated way and present to itself, it is undeniably certain.

Derrida, however, denies the possibility of this presence and in so doing removes the ground from which philosophers have in general proceeded. By denying presence, Derrida is denying that there is a present in the sense of a single definable moment which is 'now'. For most people the present is the province of the known. We may be unsure of what took place in the past, of what may take place in the future, or of what is taking place elsewhere, but we rely on our knowledge of the present, the here and now—the present perceptual world as we are experiencing it. By challenging access to the present Derrida poses a threat to both positivism and phenomenology.

Husserl made an important distinction in *The Logical Investigations* between expression and indication. The expression, linked to the intention of the speaker, is what we might call the pure meaning of the sign, and as such is distinguished from indication, which has a pointing function and could occur without any intentional meaning. Now, Derrida has argued that pure expression will always involve an indicative element. Indication can never be successfully excluded from expression. Signs cannot refer to something totally other than themselves. There is no signified which is independent of the signifier. There is no realm of meaning which can be isolated from the marks which are used to point to it.

Having argued that a realm of the independent signified does not exist, Derrida concludes, first, that no particular sign can be regarded as referring to any particular signified and, second, that we are unable to escape the system of signifiers. In combination these conclusions imply that there can be no unqualified presence.

Now, it is because of the assumption of presence that a priority has been given to speech over writing. Derrida calls this phonocentrism. Speech has been regarded as prior because it is closer to the possibility of presence. It is closer because speech implies immediacy. In speech meaning is apparently immanent, above all when, using the inner voice of consciousness, we speak to ourselves. In the moment of speech we appear to grasp its meaning and are thereby able to capture presence, as if the meaning was decided once and for all. Thus, unlike writing, which is hopelessly mediated, speech is linked to the apparent moment and place of presence and for this reason has had priority over writing. For Derrida, therefore, phonocentrism is one of the effects of presence. Derrida's attempt to deconstruct the opposition between speech and writing is linked to the uncovering of the metaphysics of presence as a whole.

Derrida has also criticized Saussure for prescribing that linguistics should be a study of speech alone rather than of speech and writing. This is an emphasis shared by Jakobson, by Lévi-Strauss, indeed by all semiological structuralists. Derrida suggests in *Of Grammatology* that this rejection of writing as an appendage, a mere technique and yet a menace built into speech—in effect, a scapegoat—is a symptom of a much broader tendency. He relates this phonocentrism to logocentrism, the belief that the first and last thing is the Logos, the Word, the Divine Mind, the *self-presence of full self-consciousness*.

Derrida suggests that Husserl found evidence for self-presence in the voice (*phone*)—not the 'real' voice, but the principle of the voice in our interior soliloquy: 'When I speak I hear myself. I hear and understand at the same time that I speak.'

In the act of speaking I seem to coincide with myself in a way quite different from what happens when I write. My spoken words seem immediately present to my consciousness and my voice becomes their intimate spontaneous medium. In writing, by contrast, my meanings threaten to escape from my control. Writing seems to rob me of my being; it is a second-hand mode of communication, a pallid mechanical transcript of speech and so always at one remove from my consciousness. It is for this reason that the Western philosophical tradition, all the way from Plato to Lévi-Strauss, has consistently vilified writing as a mere lifeless, alienated form of expression and consistently celebrated the living voice. (This will be discussed in the next section when we consider Derrida's examination of specific texts by Rousseau and Lévi-Strauss.) Behind this prejudice lies a particular view of 'man': man is able spontaneously to create and express his own meanings, to be in full possession of himself, and to dominate language as a transparent medium of his inmost being. What this traditional theory fails to see is that speaking could be just as much said to be a second-hand form of writing as writing is said to be an inferior form of speaking.

Just as Western philosophy has been 'phonocentric', centred on the 'voice' and deeply suspicious of script, so also it has been in a broader sense 'logocentric', committed to a belief in some ultimate 'word', presence, essence, truth or reality which will act as the foundation of all our thought, language and experience. It has yearned for the sign which will give meaning to all others—the 'transcendental signifier'—and for the anchoring, unquestionable meaning to which all our signs can be seen to point (the 'transcendental signified'). Examples of such signs include: God, the Idea, the World Spirit, the Self, Matter, etc. Since each of these concepts hopes to found our whole system of thought and language, it must itself be beyond that system. It cannot be implicated in the very languages which it attempts to order and anchor; it must be somehow anterior to these discourses. It must act as a linchpin or fulcrum of a whole thought-system, the sign around which all others revolve. Derrida argues that any such transcendental meaning is a fiction.

Certain meanings are elevated by social ideologies to a privileged position, for example Freedom, Authority, Order. Sometimes such meanings are seen as the *origin* of all the others, the source from which they flow. But this is a curious way of thinking, because for the meaning to have been possible other signs must already have existed. It is difficult to think of an origin without wanting to go back beyond it. At other times such meanings may be seen not as the origin but as the goal towards which all other meanings are or should be steadily marching. Teleology (thinking of things in terms of their orientation to a *telos* or end) is a way of ordering and ranking meanings in a hierarchy of significance.

Derrida labels as 'metaphysical' any thought-system which depends on an unassailable foundation, a first principle or unimpeachable ground upon which a whole hierarchy of meanings may be constructed. If you examine such first principles closely, you can see that they may always be deconstructed. First principles of this kind are commonly defined by what they exclude, by a sort of 'binary opposition'. Deconstruction is the name given to a critical operation by which such oppositions can be partially undermined.

Derrida argues that all the conceptual oppositions of

metaphysics have for ultimate reference the presence of a present. (He often uses the word 'metaphysics' as shorthand for 'being as presence'.) For Derrida the binary oppositions of metaphysics include: signifier/signified, sensible/intelligible, speech/writing, speech (*parole*)/language (*langue*), diachrony/ synchrony, space/time, passivity/activity. One of his criticisms of the structuralists, as we shall see, is that they have not put these concepts 'under erasure', that they have not put these binary oppositions into question.

Binary oppositions represent a way of seeing, typical of ideologies. Ideologies often draw rigid boundaries between what is acceptable and what is not, between self and non-self, truth and falsity, sense and non-sense, reason and madness, central and marginal, surface and depth. Derrida suggests that we should try to break down the oppositions by which we are accustomed to think and which ensure the survival of metaphysics in our thinking: matter/spirit, subject/ object, veil/truth, body/soul, text/meaning, interior/exterior, representation/presence, appearance/essence, etc. Using deconstructive methods, we can begin to unravel these oppositions a little, demonstrate how one term of an antithesis inheres within the other.

Derrida argues that phonocentrism–logocentrism relates to centrism itself—the human desire to posit a 'central' presence at beginning and end. He states that it is this longing for a centre, an authorizing pressure, that spawns hierarchized oppositions. The superior term in these oppositions belongs to presence and the logos, the inferior serves to define its status and mark a fall. The oppositions between intelligible and sensible, soul and body seem to have lasted out 'the history of Western philosophy', bequeathing their burden to modern linguistics with its opposition between meaning and word. The opposition between speech and writing takes its place within this pattern.

ROUSSEAU AND LÉVI-STRAUSS

Derrida writes that many philosophers throughout history use the opposition nature/culture. It is often stated that archaic man, living in an innocent state of nature, comes upon a danger or insufficiency of one sort or another bringing about a need or desire for community. In the evolution of human beings from nature to society the latter stage of existence is pictured as an addition to the original happy stage of nature. In other words, culture supplements nature. Before long culture comes to take the place of nature. Culture, then, functions as a supplement in two ways: it adds and it substitutes. At the same time it is potentially both detrimental and beneficial. The structure of the nature/culture opposition repeats itself in other traditional polarities: for example, health/disease, purity/contamination, good/evil, speech/writing. The first term in each opposition traditionally constitutes the privileged entity, the better state.

Derrida argues that when Rousseau describes an event or phenomenon he invariably ends up relying on the supplement. Although nature is declared to be self-sufficient it needs culture. (In a similar way education for Rousseau aids the insufficiencies of the untrained intellect.) It is suggested by Derrida that there is no original, unsupplemented nature but that nature is always already a supplemented entity. This device, *sous rature*, indicates the equivocal status of the term erased, warning, as I suggested earlier, the reader not to accept the word at face value. The marks of erasure acknowledge both the inadequacy of the terms employed—their highly provisional status—and the fact that thought simply cannot manage without them. Similarly, Derrida has a mistrust of metaphysical language but accepts the necessity to work within that language.

Rousseau believed that speech was the originary, the healthiest and the most natural condition of language; writing was merely derivative and somehow debilitating. What Derrida does (by a close analysis of Rousseau's texts, particularly the *Essay on the Origin of Languages*) is to show that Rousseau contradicts himself, so that, far from proving speech to be the origin of language—and writing merely a parasitic growth—his essay confirms the priority of writing. In other words, Rousseau's text confesses what he is at such pains to deny; his text cannot mean what it says or literally say what it means.

The theme of lost innocence is also to be found in the work of Lévi-Strauss, to which I now turn. However before I outline Derrida's criticism of Lévi-Strauss, it may be useful to go over the main features of the latter's structuralist approach. Structuralism, an attempt to isolate the general structures of human activity, found its main analogies in linguistics. It is well known that structural linguistics performs four *basic* operations: it shifts from the study of conscious linguistic phenomena to the study of their unconscious infrastructure; second, it does not treat terms as independent entities, taking instead as its basis of analysis the relations between terms; third, it introduces the concept of system; finally, it aims at discovering general laws.

What are Derrida's criticisms of structuralism? Firstly, he doubts the possibility of general laws. Secondly, he questions the opposition of the subject and the object, upon which the possibility of objective descriptions rests. In his view the description of the object is contaminated by the patterns of the subject's desire. Thirdly, he questions the structure of binary oppositions. He invites us to undo the need for balanced equations, to see if each term in an opposition is not, after all, an accomplice of the other.

The structuralism of Lévi-Strauss can be characterized as a search for invariant structures or formal universals which reflect the nature of human intelligence. This approach lends support to the traditional idea of the text as a bearer of stable meanings and the critic as a faithful seeker after truth in the text. Derrida suggests that when Lévi-Strauss describes the life of the Nambikwara and their transition to civilization he takes upon himself the burden of guilt produced by this encounter between civilization and the 'innocent' culture it ceaselessly exploits.[3] Lévi-Strauss gives expression, like Rousseau, to an eloquent longing for the lost primordial unity of speech before writing. Writing for Lévi-Strauss is an instrument of oppression, means of colonizing the primitive mind. In Derrida's view there is no pure 'authenticity' as Lévi-Strauss imagines; the theme of lost innocence is a romantic illusion.

Derrida's critique of Lévi-Strauss follows much the same path as his deconstructive readings of Saussure and Rousseau.[4] Once again it is a matter of taking a repressed theme, pursuing its textual ramifications and showing how these subvert the very order that strives to hold them in check. The 'nature' which Rousseau identifies with a pure, unmediated speech, and Lévi-Strauss with the dawn of tribal awareness, expresses nostalgia for lost innocence, an illusory metaphysics of presence which ignores the self-alienating character of all social existence.

Derrida situates the project of Lévi-Strauss (like those of Saussure and Lacan) in logocentrism. One of the central problems of anthropology is the passage from nature to culture. Derrida argues that Lévi-Strauss regularly and symptomatically ends up privileging the state of nature over culture. He appears sentimental and nostalgic, trapped in a Rousseauistic dream of innocent and natural primitive societies. Beneath the guilt and nostalgia, endemic to the field of anthropology, lies a Western ethnocentrism masking itself as liberal and humane anti-ethnocentrism.

As for writing, Lévi-Strauss conceptualizes it as a late cultural arrival, a supplement to speech, an external instrument. Speech is endowed with all the metaphorical attributes of life and healthy vitality, writing with dark connotations of violence and death.[5]

Derrida has made similar comments on Saussure. He has criticized Saussure's *Course in General Linguistics* for the sharp distinction which it maintains between the signifier and the signified, a distinction which is congruent with the traditional opposition of matter and spirit, or substance and thought. (Traditionally, this opposition has always been elaborated in ways which privilege spirit and/or thought as something that precedes matter or substance.) Derrida suggests that the distinction between signifier and signified can only be maintained if one term is believed to be final, incapable of referring beyond itself to any other term. If there is no such term, then every signified functions in turn as a signifier, in an endless play of signification.

Derrida, in short, is critical of Saussure's notion of the sign and argues that the traditional concept of signifier and signified rests firmly within the phonocentric–logocentric *episteme*. One of the characteristics of the logocentric epoch is that there is a general debasement of writing and a preference for phonetic writing (writing as imitated speech). There is, then, a rooted Western prejudice which tries to reduce writing to a stable meaning equated with the character of speech. It is widely held that in spoken language meaning is 'present' to the speaker through an act of inward self-surveillance which assures a perfect, intuitive 'fit' between intention and utterance.

Derrida demonstrates that in Saussurean linguistics privilege is granted to speech as opposed to written language. Voice becomes a metaphor of truth and authenticity, a source of self-present 'living' speech as opposed to the secondary, lifeless emanations of writing. Writing is systematically degraded and is seen as a threat to the traditional view that associates truth with self-presence. This repression of writing lies deep in Saussure's proposed methodology and shows in his refusal to consider any form of linguistic notation outside the phonetic-alphabetical script of Western culture. Against this view Derrida argues that writing is, in fact, the precondition of language and must be conceived as prior to speech. Writing is the 'free play' or element of undecidability within every system of communication.

It should be pointed out that for Derrida 'writing' does not refer to the empirical concept of writing (which denotes an intelligible system of notations on a material substance); writing is the name of the structure always already inhabited by the trace. This broadening of the term, Derrida argues, was made possible by Sigmund Freud.

FREUD AND LACAN

Derrida argues that it is no accident that when Freud tried to describe the workings of the psyche he had recourse to metaphorical models which are borrowed not from spoken language but from *writing*.[6] (This, of course, raises the question of what a text is and what the psyche must be like if it can be represented by a text.)

At first, from about the time of *Project for a Scientific*

Psychology (1895), Freud used mechanical models, but these were soon discarded. As Freud moved from neurological to psychical modes of explanation he began increasingly to refer to metaphors of optical mechanisms. Then, in *The Interpretation of Dreams* (1900), Freud thought it more appropriate to compare dreams with a system of writing than with spoken language. In order to suggest the strangeness of the logico-temporal relations in dreams Freud constantly referred to alphabetic writing as well as non-phonetic writing (pictographs, rebuses, hieroglyphics) in general. Dream symbols, he wrote, frequently have more than one or even several meanings and, as with Chinese script, the correct interpretation can only be arrived at on each occasion from the context.

Later, in *Note on the Mystic Writing Pad* (1925) Freud used a writing apparatus as a metaphor for the working of the psyche. A child's toy had come on the market under the name of Mystic Writing Pad. You may have come across a modern version of it. Basically, it consisted of a celluloid covering-sheet which rested upon a wax slab. One could write on it with a pointed stylus and the writing could be erased by raising the double covering sheet by a little pull, starting from the free lower end. The pad, cleared of writing, is thus ready to receive fresh messages. Freud argued that its construction was very much like that of the perceptual apparatus. It had an ever-ready receptive surface and could retain permanent traces of the inscriptions made on it; the wax slab, in fact, represented the unconscious.

In short, Freud found in the Mystic Writing Pad a model that would contain the problematics of the psyche—a virgin surface that still retained permanent traces. The Freudian argument is that the establishment of permanent traces in the psychic apparatus precludes the possibility of immediate perception. In other words, we have 'memory-traces', marks which are not a part of conscious memory, which may be energized into consciousness long afterwards and so affect us.

Derrida's chief interest in Freudian psychoanalysis lies in the fact that it teaches and uses a certain method of deciphering texts. Freud lists the four techniques used by the 'dream-work' of the psychic apparatus to distort or refract the 'forbidden' dream-thoughts, to produce the pictographic script of the dream: condensation, displacement, considerations of representability and secondary revision. Condensation and displacement may be rhetorically translated as metaphor and metonymy. The third item on the list refers to the technique which distorts an idea so that it can be presented as an image. Secondary revision is a psychic force that smooths over contradictions and creates an apparent connectedness.

Freud suggested that the verbal text is constituted by concealment as much as by revelation. Freud suggests that where the subject is not in control of the text, where the text looks very smooth or very clumsy, is where readers should fix their gaze. Derrida develops this further; he suggests that we should fasten upon a small but tell-tale moment in the text which harbours the author's sleight of hand and which cannot be dismissed simply as contradiction. We should examine that passage where we can provisionally locate the moment when the text transgresses the laws it apparently sets up for itself, and thus unravel—deconstruct—the very text.

Freud's greatest contemporary interpreter is Jacques Lacan. Let me briefly remind you of the key features of Lacan's thought before outlining Derrida's critique of it. Like Freud, Lacan denies that there is a difference in kind between 'the normal' and 'the abnormal'. Moreover, he rejects the work of those American psychologists who stress that the ego is the primary determinant of the psyche. In his view 'the subject' can never be a total personality and is forever divided from the object of its desire. Lacan goes on to define the unconscious in terms of the structure of a language. This extends Freud in a direction that Derrida would endorse, but, nevertheless, the relationship between these thinkers is an uneasy one.

It would seem to an outside observer that Lacan and Derrida have a lot in common: they are both deeply concerned with anti-positivist theories of language and are highly aware of language's metaphoricity. Secondly, both thinkers have been influenced by Freud's theories of the unconscious and the dream as a text. This means that they are interested in (ways of) 'reading' and (styles of) 'writing'. Thirdly, they both draw attention, as did Freud, to the relationship between nature and culture.

And so, why is there an uneasy relationship between them? Derrida argues that the goal of Lacanian analysis is to draw out and establish 'the truth' of the subject, and it appears to him that in spite of giving to the unconscious the structure of a language Lacan has entrenched some of Freud's (metaphysical) suggestions by making the unconscious the source of 'truth'. Derrida believes that Lacan sees himself as unveiling 'the true' Freud and is sceptical of Lacan's notions of 'truth' and 'authenticity', seeing them as remnants of a post-war existentialist ethic, the unacknowledged debts to Hegelian phenomenology.

Derrida believes that Lacan simplifies Freud's text. In Lacanian analysis the truth (logos) systematically shines forth as spoken or voiced. Psychoanalysis remains 'the talking cure' founded on spoken truth.[7] Derrida cautions us that when we learn to reject the notion of the primacy of the signified (of meaning over word) we should not satisfy our longing for transcendence by giving primacy to the signifier (word over meaning). He feels that Lacan has done precisely this.

I stated earlier that Derrida is attempting to subvert the logocentric theory of the sign. Traditionally, the signifier refers to the signified, that is, an acoustic image signifies an ideal concept, both of which are present to consciousness. The signifier 'dog' indicates the idea 'dog'; the real dog, the referent, is not present. In Derrida's view *the sign marks an absent presence*. Rather than present the object we employ the sign; however, the meaning of the sign is always postponed or deferred.

Derrida has developed a concept which he calls 'différance' and which refers to 'to differ'—to be unlike or dissimilar in nature, quality or form—and to 'to defer'—to delay, to postpone (the French verb *différer* has both these meanings). Spoken French makes no phonetic distinction between the endings '-ance' and '-ence'; the word registers as *différence*. This undetected difference shows up only in writing.

The advent of the concept of writing, then, is a challenge to the very idea of structure; for a structure always presumes a centre, a fixed principle, a hierarchy of meaning and a solid foundation; and it is just these notions which the endless differing and deferring of writing throws into question.

As we have seen, Derrida's analysis of Husserl led him to portray language as an endless play of signifiers. Once an independent signified was abandoned signifiers referred to other signifiers which yet again referred to signifiers. Language is thus the play of differences which are generated by signifiers which are themselves the product of those differences. Derrida incorporates into the meaning of *différance* the sense of deferring. *Différance* is itself endlessly deferred.

NIETZSCHE AND METAPHOR

Derrida's acknowledged 'precursors' were Nietzsche, Freud and Heidegger. They all felt a need for the strategy of *'sous rature'*. Heidegger put 'Being' under erasure, Freud 'the psyche', and Nietzsche 'knowing'.[8] It seems that post-structuralists such as Derrida have not so much followed in Nietzsche's footsteps as rediscovered his philosophical stance, a stance that owes its character to an all-pervasive reflexivity.

The current emphasis on reflexivity (a form of self-awareness, a turning back on oneself) is in part due to a critical shift of focus from the individual subject to the text. Thus from Nietzsche to Derrida we see the human subject—traditionally the focus of philosophical thought as the place of experience, morality, choice and will—gradually abandoned.

Derrida suggests that the main characteristics of Nietzsche's work are a systematic mistrust of metaphysics and a suspicion of the values of 'truth' and 'meaning'. Many cultural relativists believe that, although we may interpret the world differently according to our social context, there is a single world which we are all interpreting. For Nietzsche, however, there is no single, physical reality beyond our interpretations. There are only perspectives.

Rooted in Nietzsche's philosophy is the implicit stance that there are no final conclusions; the text can never be fixed and as a result it can never be deciphered either. Nietzsche believes that we are unable to escape the constraints of language and thus have no alternative but to operate within language. He is aware of the reflexive problem: if we say 'we are trapped within language and its concepts', that claim is in itself, of course, part of language. We wish to express our 'trappedness' but we are unable to do so other than in the very concepts which trap us. The original thought therefore eludes us, for if we could express it, we would not, after all, be trapped.[9]

Nietzsche, then, was deeply aware of the problem that one is bound by one's perspective. One of his ways of coping with this was by the strategy of intersubstituting opposites. If one is always bound by one's perspective, one can at least deliberately reverse perspectives as often as possible, in the process undoing opposed perspectives, showing that the two terms of an opposition are merely accomplices of each other. In this way Nietzsche problematized, for example, the opposition between 'metaphor' and 'concept', 'body' and 'mind'. I mention this because Nietzsche's undoing of opposites is rather like Derrida's undoing of them as a part of deconstructive practice.

For Nietzsche there is no possibility of a literal, true, self-identical meaning. (Derrida, too, is deeply committed to the view that philosophical discourse is something to be deciphered.) Nietzsche described the figurative drive as the impulse towards the formation of metaphors. Every idea, he said, originates through an equating of the unequal. Metaphor is the establishing of an identity between dissimilar things:

> What, therefore, is truth? A mobile army of metaphors, metonymies, anthropomorphisms; truths are illusions of which one has forgotten that they are illusions . . . coins which have their obverse effaced and now are no longer of account as coins but merely as metal.[10]

In his later work Nietzsche gave this figurative drive the

name 'will to power'. Our so-called will to truth is the will to power because the so-called drive for knowledge can be traced back to a drive to appropriate and conquer. Sometimes Nietzsche places this abstract will to power, an incessant figuration, not under the control of any knowing subject but rather in the unconscious. Indeed, for Nietzsche the important main activity is unconscious, that is, it takes place in that vast arena of the mind of which the so-called 'subject' knows nothing. Derrida has remarked that both Nietzsche and Freud questioned, often in a very similar way, the self-assured certitude of consciousness.

In many ways, then, Nietzsche anticipates both the style and the strategy of Derrida's writing. Nietzsche held that philosophy from Plato to the present had suppressed the fact that language is radically metaphorical in character. Philosophy utilized metaphors but disguised this fact. All philosophies, whatever their claim to logic or reason, rested on a shifting texture of figurative language, the signs of which were systematically repressed. In Nietzsche's view the Sophists, a school of rhetorician-philosophers in ancient Greece, came closer to wisdom by implicitly acknowledging what Socrates has to deny: that thinking is always and inseparably bound to the rhetorical devices that support it.

Following Nietzsche, Derrida makes the point that all language is ineradicably metaphorical, working by tropes and figures. It is a mistake to believe that any language is literally literal. Literary works are in a sense less deluded than other forms of discourse, because they implicitly acknowledge their own rhetorical status. Other forms of writing are just as figurative and ambiguous but pass themselves off as unquestionable truth.

One of the implications of this view is that literature can no longer be seen as a kind of poor relation to philosophy. There is no clear division between literature and philosophy, nor between 'criticism' and 'creation'. Since metaphors are essentially 'groundless', mere substitutions of one set of signs for another, language tends to betray its own fictive and arbitrary nature at just those points where it is offering to be most intensively persuasive. In short, philosophy, law, and political theory work by metaphor just as poems do, and so are just as fictional.

UNDERSTANDING METAPHOR

The study of metaphor is becoming important as it is being realized that language does not simply reflect reality but helps to constitute it. Attention is now being increasingly given to how rhetorical devices shape our experience and our judgements, how language serves to promote the possibilities of certain kinds of action and exclude the practicability of others.

In the past, metaphor was often studied as an aspect of the expressive function of language, but it is actually one of the essential conditions of speech. Language works by means of transference from one kind of reality to another and is thus essentially metaphorical. Some people have urged that technical and scientific language should be purged of metaphor but, as we have seen, metaphorical expressions are rooted in language itself. For example, we habitually think of organizations spatially, in terms of up and down. We tend to think of theories as though they were buildings, and so we talk of foundations, frameworks etc. 'Base' and 'superstructure' are fundamental concepts in Marxism. As Derrida has shown, even philosophy is permeated with metaphor without knowing it.

Meaning shifts around, and metaphor is the name of the process by which it does so. It is a threat to orderly language and allows for the proliferation of meaning. First, there is no limit to the number of metaphors for any given idea. Second, metaphor is a sort of rhetorical double-bind, which states one thing but requires you to understand something different. (I found it interesting to learn that many schizophrenics cling to the literal and avoid metaphors because these are ultimately undecidable.) Metaphors evoke relationships and the making of the relationships is very much the task of the hearer or reader. Indeed, understanding a metaphor is as much a creative endeavour as making a metaphor, and as little guided by rules. Metaphor is ubiquitous and ineradicable.

I want to stress the point that metaphors are not just the

concern of the poet or the literary critic, not just figures of speech; they represent one of the ways in which many kinds of discourse are structured and powerfully influence how we conceive things. I would like you to consider for a moment the metaphor 'time is money'. In our culture time is money in many ways; we calculate telephone calls, hourly wages, interests on loans. But not only do we *act* as if time is a valuable commodity, we also *conceive* of time that way. 'I don't have the time to give you.' 'How do you spend your time these days?' Thus we understand and experience time as the kind of thing that can be spent, wasted, budgeted, invested wisely or foolishly, saved or squandered. 'Time is money', 'time is a limited resource' and 'time is a valuable commodity' are all metaphorical concepts. They are metaphorical since we are using our everyday experiences with money, limited resources and valuable commodities to conceptualize time. But this is not the only way in which human beings may conceptualize time; it is tied to our culture. There are cultures where time is none of these things.

Let us consider another example: the organizing metaphors surrounding work and leisure. One does a full day's work; one is in or out of work. Leisure time, on the other hand, is to be filled; holiday weekends are breaks between work. We associate the metaphor of work with plenitude, with something of importance, and that of leisure with emptiness, with a vacuum. The metaphors reinforce the idea of life as first and foremost the life of work, while activities outside of it belong to the frivolous and not to the main business of life. Metaphors like these are particularly insidious since they are so interwoven into our speech that their flavour of metaphor is lost upon speakers and hearers.

THE POLITICS OF METAPHOR

Our ordinary language is saturated with metaphor. For example, in our society argument is in part structured, understood, performed and talked about in terms of war.

There is a position to be established and defended, you can win or lose, you have an opponent whose position you attack and try to destroy and whose argument you try to shoot down. The language of argument is basically, the language of physical combat. That 'argument is war' is built into the conceptual system of the culture in which we live. Lakoff and Johnson have pointed out that it need not be so; that one can easily imagine societies in which argument is conceived differently—for example as theatrical perform-ance.[11] In such a society both argument itself and the criteria for success or failure in argument would be quite unlike our own.

Some metaphors, in certain historical periods, have been liberating. The historian Christopher Hill has described how in the seventeenth century nature came to be thought of as a machine to be understood, controlled and improved upon by knowledge.[12] Nature as a machine was (at that time) a tremendously exciting, liberating idea. Human beings were freed from Providence or divine will and could not only understand the world better but could begin to change it.

I think that the creative or imaginative aspect of sociological theories often lies in their use of metaphor. Parsons likens society to a biological organism; Marx uses the metaphor of a building, the base and superstructure; Goffman uses the metaphor of a stage 'performance'. Metaphors serve to draw attention not only to similarities but to differences. As the theory develops and becomes more precise, concepts emerge that sometimes have little to do with the original metaphor.

An influential post-structuralist thinker, Michel Foucault (whose work on the social sciences and the relations between power and knowledge will be discussed in the next chapter), is particularly fond of using 'geographical' metaphors such as territory, domain, soil, horizon, archipelago, geopolitics, region, landscape. He also makes profuse use of spatial metaphors—position, displacement, site, field. Althusser, too, in *Reading Capital* uses many spatial metaphors (terrain, space, site, etc.). Foucault suggests that, since Bergson perhaps, there has been a devaluation of space. Space has been treated as the dead, the fixed, the undialectical, the immobile; time, on the contrary, was richness, fecundity, life, dialectic. But to talk in terms of space does not mean that one is hostile to time. Althusser believed that the use of spatial metaphors in his work was necessary but at the same time regressive, non-rigorous. Foucault, on the other hand, is more positive. He has said that *it is through these spatial obsessions that he came to what he was looking for*: the relations that are possible between power and knowledge. 'Once knowledge can be analysed in terms of region, domain, implantation, displacement, transposition, one is able to capture the process by which knowledge functions as a form of power and disseminates the effects of power.'[13]

I believe the metaphors determine to a large extent what we can think in any field. Metaphors are not idle flourishes—they shape what we do. They can help to make, and defend, a world view. It is important that the implications of the metaphors we employ or accept are made explicit and that the ways in which they structure our thought and even our action are better understood. I also want to stress that metaphors can be productive of new insights and fresh illuminations. They can promote unexpected or subtle parallels or analogies. Metaphors can encapsulate and put forward proposals for another way of looking at things. Through metaphor we can have an increased awareness of alternative possible worlds.

DECONSTRUCTION AND MARXISM

The metaphor most often used by deconstructionists is that of the palimpsest; reading texts resembles the X-raying of pictures which discovers, under the epidermis of the last painting, another hidden picture. Deconstructive criticism takes the 'metaphoric' structure of a text seriously. Since metaphors are not reducible to truth, their own structures 'as such' are part of the text. The deconstructive procedure is to spot the point where a text covers up its grammatical structure. Gayatri Spivak puts it like this:

If in the process of deciphering a text in the traditional way we come across a word that seems to harbour an unresolvable contradiction, and by virtue of being one word is made sometimes to work in one

way and sometimes in another and thus is made to point away from
the absence of a unified meaning, we shall catch at that word. If a
metaphor seems to suppress its implications, we shall catch at that
metaphor. We shall follow its adventures through the text coming
undone as a structure of concealment, revealing its self-transgression,
its undecidability.[14]

Derrida has provided a method of 'close-reading' a 'text'
very similar to psychoanalytic approaches to neurotic
symptoms. Deconstructive 'close-reading', having 'interrogat-
ed' the text, breaks through its defences and shows that a
set of binary oppositions can be found 'inscribed' within it.
In each of the pairs, private/public, masculine/feminine,
same/other, rational/irrational, true/false, central/peripheral,
etc., the first term is privileged. Deconstructors show that
the 'privileged' term depends for its identity on its excluding
the other and demonstrate that primacy really belongs to
the subordinate term instead.

Derrida's procedure is to examine the minute particulars of
an undecidable moment, nearly imperceptible displacements,
that might otherwise escape the reader's eye. He tries to
locate not a moment of ambiguity or irony ultimately
incorporated into the text's system of unified meaning but
rather a moment that genuinely threatens to collapse that
system. Derrida's method is not that of Hegel. Hegel's
idealist method consists in resolving by sublation the
contradictions between the binary oppositions.

Derrida stresses the point that it is not enough simply to
neutralize the binary oppositions of metaphysics. Deconstruction involves reversal and displacement. Within the familiar
philosophical oppositions there is always a violent hierarchy.
One of the two terms controls the other, holds the superior
position. The first move in deconstructing the opposition is
to overthrow the hierarchy. In the next phase this reversal
must be displaced, the winning term put 'under erasure'.
Deconstruction, then, is the attempt

> to locate the promising marginal text, to disclose the undecidable
> moment, to pry it loose with the positive lever of the signifier, to
> reverse the resident hierarchy, only to displace it; to dismantle in order
> to reconstitute what is always already inscribed.[15]

Before making some critical remarks, let me try to sum up.

Derrida has made a close study of many philosophers: Nietzsche, Rousseau, Husserl, Heidegger and others. He argues that they have been able to impose their various systems of thought only by ignoring or suppressing the disruptive effects of language. One of the ruling illusions of Western metaphysics is that reason can somehow grasp the world without a close attention to language and arrive at a pure, self-authenticating truth or method. Derrida's work draws attention to the ways in which language deflects the philosopher's project. He does this by focusing on metaphors and other figurative devices at work in the texts of philosophy. In this way Derrida underlines the rhetorical nature of philosophical arguments.

Deconstruction stresses the irreducibility of metaphor, the difference at play within the very constitution of literal meaning. It should be remembered that deconstruction is not simply a strategic reversal of categories which otherwise remain distinct and unaffected. It is an activity of reading in which texts must be read in a radically new way. There must be an awareness of ambivalence, of the discrepancy between meaning and the author's assertion. Derrida discovers a set of paradoxical themes at odds with their manifest argument. His method consists of showing how the privileged term is held in place by the force of a dominant metaphor and not, as it might seem, by any conclusive logic.[16] Metaphors often disrupt the logic of an argument.

Derrida writes that we have a metaphysical desire to make the end coincide with the means, create an enclosure, make the definition coincide with the defined, the 'father' with the 'son'; within the logic of identity to balance the equation, close the circle. In short, he is asking us to change certain habits of mind; he is telling us that the authority of the text is provisional, the origin is a trace. Contradicting logic, we must learn to use and erase our language at the same time. Derrida wants us to 'erase' all oppositions, undoing yet preserving them.

Deconstructionists tend to say that if a text seems to refer beyond itself, that reference can finally be only to another text. Just as signs refer only to other signs, texts can refer only to other texts, generating an intersecting and indefinitely expandable web called *intertextuality*. There is a proliferation of interpretations, and no interpretation can claim to be the final one. Now, Derrida is sometimes taken to be denying the possibility of truth. This is not so. It is more plausible to think of him as trying to avoid assertions about the nature of truth.

The usual superficial criticism of Derrida is that he questions the value of 'truth' and 'logic' and yet uses logic to demonstrate the truth of his own arguments. The point is that the overt concern of Derrida's writing is the predicament of having to use the resources of the heritage that he questions.

Derrida's work confronts us with many problems. Having argued that there cannot be a realm of the signified independent of the signifier, he opens up the vista of an endless play of signifiers that refer not to signifieds but to other signifiers, so that meaning is always ultimately undecidable. Derrida gives as an example of undecidability Plato's frequent presentation of writing as a drug, *pharmakon*. This Greek word can mean either 'poison' or 'cure' and, as with a drug, which way it is taken (translated) makes a lot of difference. Consider another important case of undecidability: an isolated note found amongst Nietzsche's unpublished manuscripts, a single sentence in quotation marks: 'I have forgotten my umbrella.' In a sense, we all know what this phrase means, and yet we have no idea of what its meaning is in this instance. Is it a jotting to himself, a citation, or a phrase overheard and noted for further use? Perhaps the umbrella is seen as some sort of defence, a protection from the weather? Nietzsche, on the verge of breakdown, has left his defences behind; caught in a rainstorm, he has forgotten his umbrella. Of course, it could also be analysed in Freudian terms, as psychoanalysis often focuses on the significance of forgetting and phallic objects. 'I have forgotten my umbrella': the phrase is undecidable. This illustration could be a metaphor for the whole of Derrida's text.

As we saw with Derrida's work on Saussure and Lévi-Strauss, deconstruction questions the self-identity of signifier and signified and the self-presence of the speaking subject and the voiced sign. There is an abandonment of all reference to a centre, to a fixed subject, to a privileged reference, to an origin, to an absolute founding and controlling first principle.

Deconstruction disarticulates traditional conceptions of the author and the work and undermines conventional notions of reading and history. Instead of mimetic, expressive and didactic theories of 'literature' it offers textuality (*écriture*). It kills the author, turns history and tradition into intertextuality and celebrates the reader.[17]

One of the main features of post-structuralist theory is the deconstruction of the self. In place of a unified and stable being or consciousness we get a multifaceted and disintegrating play of selves. The reader, like the text, is unstable. With deconstruction the categories 'criticism' 'philosophy' and 'literature' collapse, borders are overrun. The work, now called 'text', explodes beyond stable meaning and truth towards the radical and ceaseless play of infinite meanings. Critical writing, formerly analytical and coherent, becomes playfully fragmented.

Is this a result of Derrida's view of language? It has been suggested by Terry Eagleton that

> meaning may well be ultimately undecidable if we view language contemplatively, as a chain of signifiers on a page; it becomes 'decidable' and words like 'truth', 'reality', 'knowlege', and 'certainty' have something of their force restored to them when we think of language rather as something we *do*, as indissociably interwoven with our practical forms of life.[18]

The deconstructor's method often consists of deliberately inverting traditional oppositions and marking the play of hitherto invisible concepts that reside unnamed in the gap between opposing terms. In the move from hermeneutics and semiotics to deconstruction there is a shift of focus from identities to differences, unities to fragmentations, ontology to philosophy of language, epistemology to rhetoric, presence to absence. According to one recent commentator 'deconstruction celebrates dissemination over truth, explosion and fragmentation over unity and coherence, undecidable spaces over prudent closures, playfulness and hysteria over care and rationality.[19]

It is said that every boundary, limit, division, frame, or margin installs a line separating one entity or concept from another. That is to say, every border marks a difference. The question of the border is a question of difference. Derrida writes, 'No border is guaranteed, inside or out.' Applied to texts, this finding becomes 'no meaning can be fixed or decided upon.' According to deconstructionists there is nothing other than interpretation.[20] As there is neither an undifferentiated nor a literal bottom or ground, the activity of interpretation is endless. It is also a fact that every text tends itself to deconstruction and to further deconstruction, with nowhere any end in sight. Finally, no escape outside the logocentric enclosure is possible since the interpreter must use the concepts and figures of the Western metaphysical tradition. The term used to describe the impasse of interpretation ('there is no way out') is *aporia*. 'The supreme irony of what Derrida has called logocentrism is that its critique, deconstruction, is as insistent, as monotonous and as inadvertently systematizing as logocentrism itself.'[21]

Having given a few criticisms of Derrida and deconstruction, I now want to ask, 'Are his methods allied or opposed to Marxism?' When faced with new approaches such as deconstruction it is very hard to try to work out whether they are useful aids in building a new socialist order or are just other forms of bourgeois recuperation and domination. I think I am right in saying that deconstruction is, for Derrida, ultimately a political practice, an attempt to dismantle the logic by which a particular system of thought and, behind that, a whole system of political structures and social institutions maintains its force. But in practice it cannot be denied that his work has been grossly unhistorical and politically evasive.[22] One post-structuralist, Michel Foucault, has argued that Derrida's own decision to avoid questions about the extent to which the text arises out of and reflects underlying social practices itself reflects a social practice. He has said that by deliberately restricting himself to textual analysis the question of evaluating textual analysis as a social and political practice cannot be raised. In so far as textual undecidability precludes raising questions about truth it perpetuates the status quo.

On the other hand, some commentators have suggested that deconstruction, by unsettling the theories with which we have surrounded ourselves, serves to indicate that our account of the world *could* be different but that it cannot tell us how it would be different. Derrida seems to believe that deconstruction is able gradually to shift the structures within which we operate 'little by little to modify the terrain of our work, and thereby produce new figurations'. Is this enough? Is Derrida playing among the webs of language, 'parodying himself, and then parodying the parody'?[23]

Derrida has himself observed that certain American uses of deconstruction work to ensure 'an institutional closure' which serves the dominant political and economic interests of American society. He has also said that Marxist texts are shot through with metaphors disguised as concepts, themes that carry along with them a whole unrecognized baggage of presuppositions. But on the whole Derrida has been silent about Marx—a silence that can be construed as a prolonged postponement, a refusal as yet to engage with Marxist thought.

There are some critics, like Fredric Jameson, who feel that the claims of synchronic thought must somehow be reconciled with those of historical understanding, that there must be a *rapprochement* between rhetoric and Marxist dialectic.[24] But other critics have suggested that the Marxist model of representation, however refined in theory, is caught up in a rhetoric of tropes and images that entirely controls its logic. Christopher Norris, for example, has argued that deconstruction is inimical to Marxist thought. In his view the insights of deconstruction are inevitably couched in a rhetoric which itself lies open to further deconstructive reading: 'Once criticism enters the labyrinth of deconstruction it is committed to a sceptical epistemology that leads back to Nietzsche, rather than Marx.'[25]

Some of the most trenchant criticisms of deconstruction have been made by the English Marxist critic Terry Eagleton. According to Eagleton the main characteristics of deconstruction are that it rejects any notion of totality and that it is against the privileging of the unitary subject. Deconstructionism asserts that literary texts do not have relations to something other than themselves. It follows that deconstruction is not concerned with blaming anybody for the exploitation that exists, since this would entail some kind of vantage point from which definite judgements could be delivered. Eagleton, in 1981, wrote that

> many of the vauntedly novel themes of deconstruction do little more than reproduce some of the most commonplace topics of bourgeois liberalism. The modest disownment of theory, method and system; the revulsion from the dominative, totalising and unequivocally denotative; the privileging of plurality and heterogeneity; the recurrent gestures of hesitation and indeterminacy; the devotion to gliding and process, slippage and movement; the distaste for the definitive—it is not difficult to see why such an idiom should become so quickly absorbed within the Anglo-Saxon academies.[26]

It is suggested by Eagleton that deconstruction is not only reformist but ultra-leftist too. On the one hand, deconstruction is a sort of patient, probing reformism of the text. Because it can only imagine contradiction as the external warring of two monistic essences, it fails to comprehend class dialectics. On the other hand, deconstruction is ultra-left in that it is 'a problematic that sees meaning itself as terroristic'. Both left reformism (social democracy) and ultra-leftism are among other things antithetical responses to the failure or absence of a mass revolutionary movement.

CHAPTER 3

Foucault and the social sciences

INTRODUCTION: FOUCAULT'S VIEW OF HISTORY

Foucault is against any form of global theorizing. He wants to avoid totalizing forms of analysis and is critical of systemacity. Though his works do not constitute a system, nevertheless there is an underlying coherence which stems from the fact that Foucault's works are based on a vision of history derived from Nietzsche. Indeed, he has expressed his indebtedness to Nietzsche for having outlined a conception of history called genealogy.[1]

Nietzsche's book *On the Genealogy of Morals* was an effort to delegitimize the present by separating it from the past. This is what Foucault tries to do. Unlike the historian who traces a line of inevitability, Foucault breaks off the past from the present and, by demonstrating the foreignness of the past, relativizes and undercuts the legitimacy of the present.

Foucault rejects the Hegelian teleological model, in which one mode of production flows dialectically out of another, in favour of a Nietzschean tactic of critique through the presentation of *difference*. The Nietzschean historian begins with the present and goes backward in time until a difference is located. Then s/he proceeds forward again, tracing the transformation and taking care to preserve the discontinuities as well as the connections. This is the method used by Foucault. The alien discourses/practices are explored in such a way that their negativity in relation to the present explodes the 'rationality' of phenomena that are taken for granted.

When the technology of power of the past is elaborated in detail, present-day assumptions which posit the past as 'irrational' are undermined.

The gap between the past and the present underlines the principle of difference at the heart of Foucault's historiography. He allows the discontinuity to remain unexplained. The role of cause or explanation is severely reduced in most post-structuralist texts, since it leads to evolutionist conclusions and works against the purposes of the genealogy of difference.

Genealogical analysis, then, differs from traditional forms of historical analysis in several ways. Whereas traditional or 'total' history inserts events into grand explanatory systems and linear processes, celebrates great moments and individuals and seeks to document a point of origin, genealogical analysis attempts to establish and preserve the singularity of events, turns away from the spectacular in favour of the discredited, the neglected and a whole range of phenomena which have been denied a history. According to Foucault there has been an insurrection of subjugated knowledges, of a whole set of knowledges that have been disqualified as inadequate—naïve knowledges located low down on the hierarchy, beneath the required level of scientificity. Foucault often uses the term genealogy to refer to the union of erudite knowledge and local memories which allows us to establish a historical knowledge of struggles and to make use of this knowledge tactically today. Genealogies focus on local, discontinuous, disqualified, illegitimate knowledges against the claims of a unitary body of theory which would filter, hierarchize and order them in the name of some true knowledge.

Genealogy, I repeat, is a form of critique. It rejects the pursuit of the origin in favour of a conception of historical beginnings as lowly, complex and contingent. It attempts to reveal the multiplicity of factors behind an event and the fragility of historical forms. In this view of history, which Foucault's writings exemplify, there can be no constants, no essences, no immobile forms of uninterrupted continuities structuring the past.

REASON AND UNREASON

Foucault's early work is mainly concerned with the growth of those disciplines which are collectively known as the social or human sciences. His books are an answer to the question of how the human sciences are historically possible and what the consequences of their existence are. His studies repeatedly centre on the eighteenth century—the period in which the human sciences in their modern forms were constituted and certain new 'technologies' elaborated. Both of these developments were linked to a new philosophical conception of Man as a simultaneous subject and object of knowledge.

Throughout his life Foucault has been interested in that which reason excludes: madness, chance, discontinuity. He believes that the literary text allows 'otherness' to speak. In philosophy and law this otherness is silent, whereas in madness it is not listened to. Foucault values the literature of transgression—it attempts to subvert the constraints of all other forms of discourse by its difference. And so he admires the literary tradition that includes writers such as de Sade, Nerval, Artaud, and Nietzsche.

In his first well-known book '*Madness and Civilization*' Foucault describes how madness, along with poverty, unemployment and the inability to work, comes in the seventeenth century to be perceived as a 'social problem' which falls within the ambit of responsibility of the state.[2] There is a new conception of the state as preserver and augmenter of the general welfare. In the book there is an important discussion of the emergence of 'humanitarian' attitudes towards the insane at the end of the eighteenth century. The opening of Tuke's Retreat at York and Pinel's liberation of the insane at Bicêtre are protrayed as leading to a 'gigantic moral imprisonment', more oppressive than the former practices of brutal incarceration since they operate on the mind rather than merely on the body.

THE GREAT CONFINEMENT

At the end of the Middle Ages leprosy disappeared from the western world. Foucault suggests a connection between this and some of the attitudes then taken towards madness. As leprosy vanished a void was created and the moral values had to find another scapegoat. He shows how in the 'classical period' (1500–1800) madness attracted that stigma.

During the Renaissance madmen led an easy, wandering existence. The towns drove them outside their limits and they were allowed to wander in the open countryside. One common way of dealing with the mad was to put them on a ship and entrust them to mariners, because folly, water and sea, as everyone then 'knew', had an affinity with each other. These 'Ships of Fools' were to be found criss-crossing the seas and canals of Europe. Many texts and paintings, for example the works of Brueghel, Bosch and Dürer, refer to the theme of madness. These works of art express an enormous anxiety about the relationships between the real and the imaginary. Then, within the space of a hundred years, the 'madship' was replaced by the 'madhouse'; instead of embarkation there was *confinement*. Men did not wait until the seventeenth century to 'shut up' the mad, but it was in this period that they began to 'confine' them.

Why was this? Foucault argues that during the second half of the seventeenth century social sensibility, common to European culture, began to manifest itself; a 'sensibility to poverty and to the duties of assistance, new forms of reaction to the problems of unemployment and idleness, a new ethic of work'.[3] And so, enormous houses of confinement (sometimes called 'houses of correction') were created throughout Europe. To these places a (strangely) mixed group of people, poor vagabonds, the unemployed, the sick, the criminals, and the insane were sent. No differentiation was made between them.

Confinement was a massive phenomenon, a 'police' matter whose task was to suppress beggary and idleness as a source of disorder.

The unemployed person was no longer driven away or punished; he was taken in charge, at the expense of the nation but at the cost of his individual liberty. Between him and society an implicit system of obligation was established: he had the right to be fed, but he must accept the physical and moral constraint of confinement.[4]

The repressive function of the houses of confinement was combined with a new use: the internees were made to work. In the Middle Ages the great sin had been pride, in the seventeenth century it was sloth. Since sloth had become the absolute form of rebellion, the idle were forced to work. Labour was instituted as an exercise in moral reform. Confinement played a double role: it absorbed the unemployed in order to mask their poverty and it also avoided the social or political disadvantages of agitation.

In the Renaissance madness had been present everywhere, but the houses of confinement hid it away. Confinement marked a decisive event: 'The new meanings assigned to poverty, the importance given to the obligation to work, and all the ethical values that are linked to labour, ultimately determined the experience of madness and inflected its course.'[5] Most of Foucault's book is a detailed description of how madness was thought about in the seventeenth and eighteenth centuries: he writes about mania and melancholia, hysteria and hypochondria; how it was thought that the savage danger of madness was related to the danger of the passions, and how madness was conceived as a form of animality to be mastered only by discipline.

Gradually in the eighteenth century confinement came to be seen as a gross error; it began to be said that charity was a cause of impoverishment and that vagabonds should seek employment. Moreover, legislators were beginning to be embarrassed because they no longer knew where to place mad people—in prison, hospital or the family. Measured by their functional value alone, the houses of confinement were a failure: when the unemployed were herded into forced-labour shops, there was less work available in neighbouring regions and so unemployment increased. Thus the houses of confinement, a social precaution clumsily formulated by a nascent industrialization, disappeared throughout Europe at the beginning of the nineteenth century.

THE BIRTH OF THE ASYLUM

The legislation passed to segregate criminals and poor people from fools was prompted, as often as not, by a desire to protect the poor and the criminal from the frightening bestiality of the madman. A hallowed tradition has associated Tuke in England and Pinel in France with the liberation of the insane and the abolition of constraint. But, Foucault argues, we must be sceptical of this claim. In fact, Tuke created an asylum where the partial abolition of physical constraint was part of a system whose essential element was the constitution of a self-restraint. 'He substituted for the free terror of madness the stifling anguish of responsibility .... The asylum no longer punished the madman's guilt, it is true, it did more, it organized that guilt.'[6]

The Quaker Samuel Tuke organized his Retreat so that it had a religious ethos. In it work was imposed as a moral rule, a submission to order. Instead of repression there was surveillance and judgement by 'authority'. Everything at the asylum was arranged so that the insane were transformed into minors and given rewards and punishments like children. A new system of education was applied; first the inmates were to be subjugated, then encouraged, then applied to work: 'The asylum would keep the insane in the imperative fiction of the family; the madman remains a minor, and for a long time reason will retain for him the aspect of the Father.'[7]

During the 'classical period' poverty, laziness, vice, and madness mingled in an equal guilt within unreason. Madness during the nineteenth century began to be categorized as social failure. The doctor gained a new social status and increasingly the patient surrendered to the medical profession. In short, the asylum of the age of positivism was not a free realm of observation, diagnosis and therapeutics. In the hands of Tuke and Pinel it became a juridical space where one was accused, judged and condemned—an instrument of moral uniformity. Invoking the names of those who have gone mad, such as Artaud, Hölderlin, Nerval, Nietzsche, and van Gogh, Foucault reminds us that we are in the habit of calling this gigantic moral imprisonment the 'liberation' of the insane.

Foucault's book has a sense of great loss. It states that during the Middle Ages mad people were not locked up; indeed they possessed a certain freedom. There was a notion of the 'wise fool'—like the character in *King Lear*. Even in the eighteenth century madness had still not lost its power; but in the nineteenth century the dialogue between reason and unreason was broken. There is now only the monologue of reason *on* madness. Foucault suggests that there are dimensions that are missing in reason or, to put it in another way, there may be a wisdom in madness.

Human beings have been released from the physical chains, but these have been replaced by mental ones. One of the main themes of the book is how external violence has been replaced by internalization. The birth of the asylum can be seen as an allegory on the constitution of subjectivity. It is an indictment of modern consciousness. *Madness and Civilization* is as much concerned with the plight of everyday consciousness in the modern world as with the specific fate of those labelled insane. Foucault implies that modern forms of public provision and welfare are inseparable from ever tighter forms of social and psychological control. From the beginning, intervention and administrative control have defined the modern state.

According to Foucault madness can never be captured; madness is not exhausted by the concepts we use to describe it. His work contains the Nietzschean idea that there is more to madness than scientific categorization; but in associating freedom with madness he seems to me to romanticize madness. For Foucault to be free would be *not* to be a rational, conscious being. Though Foucault's position is a relativist one, he actually has deep-seated preferences. Critics of Foucault have asked, 'How can Foucault capture the spirit of madness when he is so obviously writing from the viewpoint of reason?'[8] Shouldn't he, logically, give up writing altogether?

Most of Foucault's books are really analyses of *the process of modernization*. One of the characteristics of his work is the tendency to condense a general historical argument into a tracing of the emergence of specific institutions. His second main work, *The Birth of the Clinic*, is subtitled 'An Archaeology of Medical Perception'.[9] This perception or 'gaze' is formed by the new, untrammelled type of observation made possible for the doctor at the bedside of the hospitalized patient intersecting with a system of monitoring the state of health of the nation through the new teaching hospital.

Foucault's subsequent books, *The Order of Things* and *The Archaeology of Knowledge*, deal largely with the structure of scientific discourses.[10] (Discourses are perhaps best understood as practices that systematically form the objects of which they speak.) Foucault is concerned with the question, what set of rules permit certain statements to be made?

In *The Order of Things* Foucault argues that in certain empirical forms of knowledge such as biology, psychiatry, medicine, etc. the rhythms of transformation do not follow the continuist schemas of development which are normally accepted. In medicine, for example, within a period of about twenty-five years there arose a completely new way of speaking and seeing. How is it that at certain moments and in certain knowledges there are these sudden transformations? There seem to be changes in the rules of formation of statements which are accepted as scientifically true. There is a whole new 'regime' of discourse which makes possible the separation not of the true from the false but of what may be characterized as scientific from what may not be characterized as scientific.

Unlike most of Foucault's other work, *The Order of Things* and *The Archaeology of Knowledge* are not concerned with the emergence of modern forms of administration. One reason for this may be that the structuralists during the 1960s veered away from any form of political analysis and that he was influenced by them.

Looking back on his early work, Foucault concedes that

what was missing was a consideration of the effects of power:

> When I think back now, I ask myself what else it was that I was talking about, in *Madness and Civilization* or *The Birth of the Clinic*, but power? Yet I'm perfectly aware that I scarcely ever used the word and never had such a field of analysis at my disposal.[11]

In his later work, where Foucault is concerned with power and knowledge, he is much more inclined to talk about 'apparatuses'. An apparatus is a structure of heterogeneous elements such as discourses, laws, institutions, in short, the said as much as the unsaid. The apparatus contains strategies of relations of forces supporting, and supported by, types of knowledge.

A STRUGGLE OVER MEANING

Foucault returned to some of the topics discussed in *Madness and Civilization* in a book which he edited twelve years later called *I, Pierre Rivière . . . A Case of Parricide in the 19th Century*.[12] One of the main themes of this 'dossier' is the problematic division between the innocence of unreason and the guilt of crime. This work is truly interdisciplinary in that one can approach it from the point of view of history, politics, literature, psychiatry, or the law.

It raises many important questions about these forms of knowledge and their interrelationship. The case of Pierre Rivière marked the border where many types of discourse, institutions and powers confronted one another. To anyone wishing to read a case study of a struggle over meaning or wanting to understand what Foucault means by a 'battle among discourses through discourses' I would recommend this book.

Pierre Rivière was, in two different ways but in virtually a single deed, an 'author'. In 1835 the twenty-year-old peasant killed his mother, his sister and his brother. While he was detained he wrote a memoir giving particulars and an explanation of the crime. Though he had received only a village education he produced a text that has beauty and eloquence. The memoir is of interest to historians and others because it raises so many questions. Frightful crimes were being committed in the countryside at that time, but what were those acts saying and why did they speak such a terrifying language? Why was parricide equated with regicide?

The life story of this obscure peasant (who resembles Julien Sorel) has considerable literary value; and as there are so many interpretations it raises the question, 'How do we read a text?' What is fascinating is that the book shows how two conflicting arguments (that advanced by the doctors and that put forward by the lawyers) could be constructed from two different accounts of Rivière's life, both of them based on the *same* sources of information. Of course, the frontier between rationality and madness is hard to establish, but can they coexist in the form of a partial delusion and the lucid interval? While some people saw in Rivière's memoir a proof of rationality and therefore wanted to condemn him to the guillotine, other people saw in the memoir a sign of madness and hence wanted to isolate him in an asylum.

Some said that the same signs of madness could be found alike in the fact of premeditated murder and in the particulars of what was narrated; others said that the same signs of lucidity could be found both in the *preparation and circumstances* of the murder and in the fact that Rivière had written it down. In other words, the fact of killing and the fact of writing, the deeds done and the things narrated, coincided since they were elements of a like nature.

While the doctors presented Rivière as always having been mad, the lawyers claimed that he was always sane. The doctors stressed his 'bizarre behaviour' as a sign of his madness; lawyers, by stressing Rivière's intelligence, ascribed to him full responsibility for his crime. What was really happening in this competition between the medical and the penal authorities was an attempt to pathologize a sector of criminality. Emergent psychiatry was attempting to gain a space for its intervention and create a new apparatus. There is an interesting section in the book on how the development of the theory of limited responsibility, the existence of extenuating circumstances, opened the way in introducing not merely psychiatry but all the social and human sciences, psychology, sociology, genetics and so on, into judicial procedure.

This book, then, gives us an idea of how a particular kind of knowledge such as medicine or psychiatry is formed. Foucault tells us that the documents in the book give us a key to the relations of power, domination and conflict within which discourses emerge and function, and hence provide material for a potential analysis of discourse which may be both tactical and political and therefore strategic. In short, the book exemplifies one of Foucault's main preoccupations: the attempt to rediscover the interaction of discourses as weapons of attack and defence in the relations of power and knowledge.

DISCIPLINARY POWER

I have mentioned several times that Foucault's work owes much to Nietzsche. Many of the themes that have reappeared in post-structuralism, such as relativism and the relationship between knowledge and power, can be found in Nietzsche's work. Foucault inverts, following Nietzsche, the common-sense view of the relation between power and knowledge. Whereas we might normally regard knowledge as providing us with power to do things that without it we could not do, Foucault argues that knowledge is a power over others, the power to define others. In his view knowledge ceases to be a liberation and becomes a mode of surveillance, regulation, discipline.

Foucault's masterpiece *Discipline and Punish* focuses on the moment when it became understood that it was more efficient and profitable to place people under surveillance than to subject them to some exemplary penalty. This transition in the eighteenth century corresponds to the formation of a new mode of exercise of power.[13] The book begins with a horrifying description of a regicide's torture and public execution. The author then describes how within eighty years vast changes occurred: torture disappeared, there was regulation of prisoners, and the new mechanisms of surveillance began to be applied in barracks, hospitals, prisons and schools.

Foucault suggests that under a feudal and monarchical system individualization is greatest at the summit of society. Power is visibly embodied in the person of the king, who has unlimited power over an anonymous body of subjects. Under this type of regime the notion of crime is still not fully distinguished from that of sacrilege, so that punishment takes the form of a ritual intended not to 'reform' the offender but to express and restore the sanctity of the law which has been broken. In general, power in feudal societies tends to be haphazard and imprecise, whereas in modern societies the agencies of punishment become part of a pervasive, impersonal system of surveillance and correction which pays an ever-increasing attention to the psychology of the individual. Intention rather than transgression now becomes the central criterion of culpability.

Let me restate Foucault's argument. In feudal societies, under *monarchical power*, the judiciary only arrested a very small proportion of criminals and it was argued that punishment must be spectacular so as to frighten the others. The new theorists of the eighteenth century objected to this: such a form of power was too costly in proportion to its results. In contrast to monarchical power, there is *disciplinary power*, a system of surveillance which is interiorized to the point that each person is his or her own overseer. Power is thus exercised continuously at a minimal cost.

Once you suppress the idea of vengeance, which previously was the act of a sovereign threatened in his very sovereignty by the crime, punishment can only have a meaning within a technology of reform. Foucault's hypothesis is that the prison was linked from its beginning to a project for the transformation of individuals. The failure of the project was immediate and this was realized virtually from the start. People knew that prisons did not reform but on the contrary manufactured criminals and criminality. It was soon discovered that criminals could be put to good use as informers, pimps, policemen. Foucault writes that at the end of the eighteenth century people dreamed of a society without crime. And then the dream evaporated. Crime was too useful to dream of anything as dangerous as a society without crime. 'No crime means no police. What makes the presence and control of the police tolerable for the population, if not fear of the criminal?'[14] In short, supervised illegality was directly useful. It provided a justification and a means for the general surveillance, the policing of the entire population.

The transformation of Western societies from monarchical (or sovereign) power to disciplinary power is epitomized in Foucault's description of the Panopticon, an architectural device advocated by Jeremy Bentham towards the end of the eighteenth century. In this circular building of cells no prisoner can be certain of not being observed from the central watch-tower, and so the prisoners gradually begin to police their own behaviour.

This new mode of power, which we can call panopticism, was used first of all in schools, barracks and hospitals. People learned how to establish dossiers, systems of marking and classifying. Then there was the permanent surveillance of a group of pupils or patients; and at a certain moment in time these methods began to be generalized.

If you have already read *Discipline and Punish* you will have noticed the likeness between the Panopticon (the 'all-seeing') and the Christian God's infinite knowledge. It is also similar to Freud's concept of the super-ego as the internal monitor of unconscious wishes. Another parallel is between the Panopticon and the computer monitoring of individuals in advanced capitalism. Foucault hints that the new techniques of power were needed to grapple with the increase in population: to undertake its administration and control because of newly-arising problems of public health, hygiene, housing conditions, longevity, fertility, sex. As we shall see in a moment, sex is politically significant because it is located at the point of intersection of the discipline of the body and the control of the population.

At times *Discipline and Punish* regresses to a totalizing

logic in which the Panopticon becomes the model for all forms of domination. Moreover, though Foucault makes a powerful case against the modern prison system, he offers nothing as a constructive alternative to it. One point that puzzles me is that, according to Foucault, the Panopticon is a machine in which everyone is caught and which no one knows. What, then, is the origin of this strategy, how do these tactics arise? Foucault does not give a clear answer; he merely states that all these tactics were invented and organized from the starting points of local conditions and particular needs, that they took shape in piecemeal fashion, prior to any class strategy.

TECHNICAL RATIONALITY

What is the problem that really worries Foucault? Bourgeois thought stresses the idea of the conscious subject who calculates means and ends. The subject is rational, autonomous and capable of initiating action. But the more autonomous one becomes the more important the criterion of means and ends becomes. Now, the work of Foucault has often been compared with that of Max Weber, one of whose central themes was rationalization. Weber held that action could be rational in its ends or its means. Bureaucracies stressed efficiency of means. In impersonal, bureaucratic organizations reason was shaped into scientific rationality. The objective of scientific rationality is to gain mastery over the physical and the social environment. Weber, following Nietzsche, argued that scientific rationality focused on means but not on ends. Instrumental reason cannot tell us anything about how to live our lives. In a sense Foucault reiterates the fears of (Nietzsche and) Weber: science uncovers the mythology in the world; but science itself is a myth which has to be superseded. Scientific knowledge has brought about a disenchantment with the world. Means can be calculated with efficiency—this is what is called technical rationality—but ends, values, become increasingly problematic to determine. One effect of the rise of technical or instrumental rationality is the process of reification which has produced disenchantment.

This analysis is in some ways close to the one made by the 'critical theorists' of the Frankfurt School. Theodor Adorno and Max Horkheimer, much influenced by Weber, analysed the capitalist economy as merely one form of the autonomous dynamic of a means–end rationality. This makes possible not only an unprecedented increase in the forces of production, and therefore in the domination of external nature, but also in the domination of human beings who are adapted to the system of production through social engineering and psychological manipulation. According to Adorno and Horkheimer the calculating instrumental rationality required of the subject in its struggle to gain independence from the overwhelming powers of external nature requires a corresponding repression of the spontaneity of inner nature.[15] For Weber and the Frankfurt School the social forms engendered by (technical or) instrumental rationality represent a profounder threat to human freedom than class oppression. Adorno and Horkheimer believed that even the space for individual responsibility and initiative, which was opened during the early phases of capitalism, is now closed by the administered society.

Foucault, too, is worried about the productivity and efficiency of those instrumental–rational forms of organization which Weber detected in modern bureaucracies and in the capitalist organization of the labour process. Foucault's view that power cannot be considered a possession of groups or individuals should be understood in the light of Weber's account of the transition from 'traditional' to 'legal–rational' forms of domination. That is to say, power in modern societies does not depend upon the prowess and prestige of individuals but is exercised through an impersonal administrative machinery operating in accordance with abstract rules.

SEXUALITY AND POWER

Foucault is generally known as the historian who stresses discontinuities. But in fact, when he writes about other thinkers he often emphasizes the continuities in their work. For example, at the time Althusser was emphasizing the epistemological break in Marx's work (separating the early 'ideological' texts from the later anti-humanist, economic work) Foucault argued that Marx's concepts were only a development of those of David Ricardo and, what is more, that Marxism fitted into nineteenth-century thought like a fish in water; that is, it was unable to breathe anywhere else. Similarly, Freud's work does not represent a radical break; psychoanalysis is, in fact, an episode in the machinery of the confession. (By confession Foucault means all those procedures by which subjects are incited to produce a discourse of truth about their sexuality which is capable of having effects on the subjects themselves.) In the usual histories one reads that sexuality was ignored by medicine and psychiatry and that at last Freud discovered the sexual origin of neuroses. Now everyone knows, says Foucault, that that is not true; the problem of sexuality was massively inscribed in the medicine and psychiatry of the nineteenth century.

Psychoanalysis was established in opposition to a certain kind of psychiatry, the psychiatry of degeneracy, eugenics and heredity. In relation to that psychiatry psychoanalysis played a liberating role; some of its activities, however, have the function of control and normalization. In Foucault's view psychoanalysis grew out of the institutionalization of confessional procedures which has been so characteristic of our civilization. Viewed over a shorter span of time, it forms part of that medicalization of sexuality which is another phenomenon of the West.

These are some of the views expressed in *The History of Sexuality; Volume One: An Introduction*.[16] One of the main points of the book is that sexuality is far more a positive product of power than power was ever repression of sexuality. Foucault states that we have only had sexuality since the eighteenth century, and sex since the nineteenth. What we had before that was, no doubt, the flesh.

Foucault argues that at one time the Christian confession was the locus of sexuality. In the Middle Ages the priest was concerned with what people did; the faithful were asked in detail about their sexual activities. In that period sexuality, in the understanding of society, concerned only the body. With the Reformation and the Counter-Reformation the discourse on sexuality takes another form. In the confession the priest begins to inquire not only about actions but also about intentions. Sexuality begins to be defined in terms of the mind as well as the body. This is similar to the pattern of change discovered by Foucault in his history of crime and punishment; there also, discourse intensifies from a concern with action and the body to a concern with the mind and its intentions.

Foucault's work shows how in the eighteenth century processes of training and regulation of human bodies emerged in a wide range of specific institutional locations: in factories, prisons and schools. The overall outcome of these disciplinary practices were bodies that were useful and docile, productive and subjected. And then, at the beginning of the twentieth century, the discourse on sex became a matter of science. Foucault's main example of a modern discourse on sexuality, a new scientific confessional, is psychoanalysis. He says that by positing a sexual instinct Freud opened up a new realm for the domination of science over sexuality.

Foucault draws attention to the dissolution of the forms of group identity characteristic of traditional societies, and their replacement by a form of identity which depends increasingly upon the capacity of the individual to reflect upon and articulate the domain of private experience. It is an attack on what he calls 'the repressive hypothesis', the assumption that the asceticism and work discipline of bouregois society demanded a repression of sexuality. The sexual-repression hypothesis is associated with Wilhelm Reich and the Frankfurt School. Reich's story, to put it simply, is that with the onset of capitalism there was an increasing repression and confinement of (natural) human

sexuality. The authoritarian bourgeois father, devoted obsess-
ively to accumulating capital, hoarded his energies for the
market place and the factory. Foucault's *The History of
Sexuality* opens with an attack on this Freudo-Marxist
position. He claims that it was precisely during this period
that there was 'a veritable explosion' of discourses about
sexuality in, for example, medical, psychiatric and educational theories and the practices that were both informed
and presupposed by these discourses.

Foucault's main objection to the repressive hypothesis is
its reliance upon a negative conception of power as
prohibition or limitation. Against this he maintains that
since the eighteenth century power has become increasingly
positive or productive, involving the careful construction of
new capacities rather than the repression or removal of pre-
existing ones. The fundamental thesis of the book is that
sexuality is not a natural reality but the product of a system
of discourses and practices which form part of the intensifying
surveillance and control of the individual. Foucault suggests
that liberation is a form of servitude, since our apparently
'natural' sexuality is in fact a product of power.

Foucault's primary objective is to provide a critique of
the way modern societies control and discipline their
populations by sanctioning the knowledge claims and
practices of the human sciences: medicine, psychiatry,
psychology, criminology, and sociology. The human sciences
have established certain norms and these are reproduced
and legitimized through the practices of teachers, social
workers, doctors, judges, policemen and administrators. The
human sciences have made man a subject of study and a
subject of the state. There has been an unrelenting expansion
of rationalized systems of administration and social control.
It is time to examine Foucault's theory of power.

POWER AND KNOWLEDGE

In structuralism all relations were seen as linguistic, symbolic,
discursive. After a while such a linguistic model was seen

to be limited and some theorists became increasingly interested in power. Foucault's writings are an example of this trend. His work in the 1960s focused on language and the constitution of the subject in discourse. The individual subject was an empty entity, an intersection of discourses. In his later work Foucault has shifted from linguistic determination to the view that individuals are constituted by power relations, power being the ultimate principle of social reality.

Foucault has remarked that Nietzsche's contemporary presence is increasingly important. It was Nietzsche who specified the power relation as the general focus, whereas for Marx it was the production relation. Nietzsche is the philosopher of power, a philosopher who managed to think of power without having to confine himself within a political theory in order to do so. Historians have studied those who held power and there have been many anecdotal histories of kings and generals; contrasted with this there has been the history of economic processes. Again distinct from this we have histories of institutions. But power in its strategies and its mechanisms has never been studied. What has been studied even less is the relation between power and knowledge. It is, of course, the interdependence of power and knowledge (*pouvoir–savoir*) that constitutes the strategic fulcrum of Foucault's later work.

Traditionally, power has often been thought of in negative terms and been seen as an essentially judicial mechanism: as that which lays down the law, which limits, obstructs, refuses, prohibits and censors. It presupposes a sovereign whose role is to forbid: to have power is to say no. And the challenging of power thus conceived can appear only as transgression.

This is the view that Foucault accepted in his early work; but by around 1971–2 he realized that the question of power needed to be reformulated. He replaced a judicial, negative conception of power with a technical and strategic one. This positive view can be seen in *Discipline and Punish* and *The History of Sexuality*. Modern power operates through the construction of 'new' capacities and modes of activity rather than through the limitation of pre-existing ones.

Foucault argues that power is not a possession or a capacity.[17] It is not something subordinate to or in the service of the economy. He insists that relations of power do not emanate from a sovereign or a state; nor should power be conceptualized as the property of an individual or class. Power is not simply a commodity which may be acquired or seized. Rather it has the character of a network; its threads extend everywhere. Foucault suggests that an analysis of power should concentrate not on the level of conscious intention but on the point of application of power. In other words, he wants to shift attention from questions such as 'Who has power?' or 'What intentions or aims do power holders have?' to the processes by which subjects are constituted as effects of power.

He rejects analyses which locate the source of origin of power within a structure or an institution at a centre or summit. Foucault's view calls into question the Marxist notion of conflict between a ruling class and a subordinate class. Foucault states that the mechanisms, techniques and procedures of power were not invented by the bourgeoisie, were not the creation of a class seeking to exercise effective forms of domination; rather they were deployed from the moment that they revealed their political and economic utility for the bourgeoisie.

For Foucault, then, conceiving of power as repression, constraint or prohibition is inadequate: power 'produces reality'; it 'produces domains of objects and rituals of truth'. Foucault remarks that we often hear the cliché 'power makes mad', but we should consider the fact that the exercise of power itself creates and causes to emerge new objects of knowledge. Conversely, knowledge induces effects of power. It is not possible for power to be exercised without knowledge, it is impossible for knowledge not to engender power.

FOUCAULT AND ALTHUSSER

Foucault's thesis that subjects are constituted by power derives from Nietzsche (who remarked that an internalized moral control of behaviour can only be inculcated through threats and violence).[18] Like Nietzsche Foucault analyses the transition from a state of overt violence and brutality to a condition of internalized restraint. As I said earlier, Foucault argues that the physical confinement and repression that occurred in the sixteenth, seventeenth and eighteenth centuries left a greater power and freedom to madness than modern methods of treatment, which aim at transforming the consciousness of the insane. Where formerly there had been the 'free terror of madness' there now reigns the 'stifling anguish of responsibility'. This regime of incessant observation and judgement forms the conditions for the internalization of morality. As Peter Dews has observed, what Foucault is really talking about here is not the specific regime of the modern asylum but the makings of modern subjectivity.[19]

Foucault is against the philosophical tradition which takes for granted that human subjects are responsible and autonomous. He is critical of the notion of the subject throughout his work. You will remember that in *Discipline and Punish* Foucault wrote that the Panopticon creates subjects responsible for their own subjection. Self-enslavement is the moment of horror. The book can be read as a parable about human subjectivity. At one time the ruler was individualized and the mass was anonymous. Now the bureaucracy is anonymous and the subject is individualized. Foucault is ambiguous about whether the Panopticon is power or an apparatus of power. He believes, like Althusser, that ideology will not end in the future, that there will never be a transparent society.

It could be argued that Foucault's notion of the Panopticon is in some ways rather like Althusser's account of ideology. In Althusser there are many small subjects in subordinate positions in relation to the absolute subject.[20] Similarly, in Foucault there are many separate, individual prisoners who are subject to 'the look', the gaze. The inmates in the circular building do not know when they are being observed from the central tower, and so they tend to behave as if they were always under surveillance.

I think this may be a good place to consider some of the similarities—and the differences—between Foucault and Althusser that are often overlooked but which are really quite important. One of the most obvious similarities is their *anti-humanist* approach. You may remember that Althusser attempted to make a distinction between ideology and science and argued that humanism has an ideological character. Let me quickly distinguish some of the characteristic features of humanism. There is, firstly, the Cartesian notion of the subject: 'I think, therefore I am. I have intentions, purposes, goals, therefore I am the sole source and free agent of my actions.' Humanism is also associated with 'methodological individualism' (the idea that societies consist only of individuals). Humanism is sometimes accompanied by the belief that social relations in a socialist society will be transparent. Anti-humanists argue that unconditional emancipation is a fantasy—and that fantasies are dangerous. Althusser and Foucault regard humanism as an error; and yet there is the irony that, in a sense, we are all humanists. We experience the world as humanists, but this is not necessarily the way we theorize.

Another similarity between Althusser and Foucault is that they both emphasize the necessity of applying certain anti-humanist theories to the reading of texts. It must be said, however, that just as there is no clear way of deciding what is idealist and what is materialist, there is no simple way of deciding what is humanist and what is anti-humanist.[21] Thirdly, both Althusser and Foucault have produced work that raises problems rather than provides solutions. Althusser's books *For Marx* and *Reading Capital* are good examples of this.[22] Many of Foucault's writings are polemical and his concepts are unstable because of their provisional character.

Indeed, Foucault is often depicted as some sort of freewheeling relativist in contrast to Althusser, the guardian of Marxist truth; but it has been argued by Mark Cousins and Athar Hussain that both Foucault and Althusser are against a rigid notion of truth and falsity.[23] One of

Althusser's main points is that science produces its own objects and that it is itself the product of social practices. Foucault argues that the character of the knowledge of the human sciences is different from that of the natural sciences. In the human sciences (what Foucault calls) Man is both subject and object.

There are also many *differences* between Foucault and Althusser which must be remembered. Althusser is committed by his espousal of Marxist materialism both to a strong view of the mind-independent reality of the objects of scientific knowledge *and* to a positive valuation of the cognitive authority of science. Ted Benton has perceptively suggested that many of the inner tensions and oscillations in Althusser's work stem from his difficulties in synthesizing the French epistemological tradition, which stresses that knowledge is culturally produced, with Marxist materialism with its stress on the existence of a mind-independent reality.[24]

Althusser makes a sharp distinction between ideology and science. He believes that, historically, ideology precedes the science, that is produced when there is an 'epistemological break', but that it survives alongside science as an essential element of every social formation. Foucault, however, rejects the concept of ideology. What he tries to do is to talk about the social function of ideology but without an epistemological dimension; it is as if he did not want to get trapped in the interminable debates about reality and illusion.

What are Foucault's objections to the concept of ideology? In Marxist thought ideology is usually conceived as a form of mystification; it does not have the status of scientific knowledge. From Foucault's Nietzschean viewpoint, however, all discourses are merely perspectives. I think Foucault's objection to the concept of ideology derives from his anti-humanism. The humanist notion of ideology places the sources of ideas in subjects, but Foucault's project is not to study Man but the mechanisms of the human sciences. He believes that by taking a point of view other than that of the subject one can decipher the mechanisms through which the human sciences come to dominate, not liberate, the subject. Furthermore, Foucault is opposed to the central feature of historical materialism upon which the concept of ideology rests: the distinction between base and superstructure. He believes that ideas are not reducible to the mode of production. In his view discourses are already powers and do not need to find their material force somewhere else, as in the mode of production. Let us look in more detail at Foucault's criticisms of Marxism.

FOUCAULT'S CRITIQUE OF MARXISM

Foucault is very concerned about the inhibiting effect of global, totalitarian theories (Marxism and psychoanalysis) and argues that the attempt to think in terms of a totality has in fact proved a hindrance to research. As I mentioned earlier, Foucault believes that Marx's analysis of the formation of capital is for a large part governed by the concepts he derives from the framework of Ricardian economics. In short, Marx did not escape from the epistemological space established by Ricardo.[25]

What are Foucault's criticisms of the Marxist conception of the state and of the revolutionary movement? Firstly, in order to be able to fight a state which is more than just a government, the revolutionary movement must possess equivalent politico-military forces and hence must constitute itself as a party, organized internally in the same way as a state apparatus with the same mechanisms of hierarchies and structures of power. This consequence is heavy with significance. Secondly, during the period of the dictatorship of the proletariat the state apparatuses must be kept sufficiently intact for them to be employed against the class enemy. In order to operate these state apparatuses which have been taken over but not destroyed it is necessary to use specialists from the bourgeoisie. (This is what happened in the USSR.) But, Foucault argues, power is not localized in the state apparatuses and nothing in society will be changed if the mechanisms of power that function outside, below and alongside the state apparatuses on a much more minute and everyday level are not also changed.

Power is not located in the state apparatus; it passes through much finer channels and is much more ambiguous, since each individual has at his or her disposal at least some power. Moreover, it should be remembered that the reproduction of the relations of production is not the only function served by power. The systems of domination and the circuits of exploitation certainly interact, intersect and support each other, but they do not coincide. Excessive insistence on the state playing an exclusive role leads to the risk of overlooking all the mechanisms and effects of power which do not pass directly via the state apparatus, yet often sustain the state more effectively than its own institutions. In fact, the state can only function on the basis of other already existing power networks such as the family, kinship, knowledge, and so forth. Of course, the critics of Foucault argue against this position because in their opinion he neglects the state and focuses only on the micro-powers that are exercised at the level of daily life.

Foucault is deeply antagonistic to the Marxist concept of ideology; he says that it is difficult to make use of it for three reasons. Firstly, it always stands in virtual opposition to something else which is supposed to count as truth. What interests him, of course, is how effects of truth are produced within discourses which in themselves are neither true nor false. Secondly, analyses which prioritize ideology trouble him because they always presuppose a human subject on the lines of the model provided by classical philosophy. Foucault wants to dispense with the constituent subject. Thirdly, ideology stands in a secondary position relative to something which functions as its base, as its material economic determinant. Perhaps I should add here that Foucault is also highly critical of the concept 'repression', which he regards as negative, psychological and insufficiently analytical. What makes power accepted is that it not only weighs on us as a force that says no, but it produces things: it induces pleasure, forms of knowledge, produces discourse.

Foucault has little to say about class consciousness, class ideology, class interest or class struggle for the simple reason that he does not believe in class. He writes '. . . one should not assume a massive and primal condition of domination, a binary structure with "dominators" on one side and "dominated" on the other, but rather a multiform production of relations of domination . . . .'[26]

Foucault therefore stresses the importance of *local, specific struggles* and believes that they can have effects and implications which are not simply professional or sectoral. In his view the universal intellectual (usually a writer), the bearer of values in which all can recognize themselves, has become outmoded. Intellectuals now tend to work within specific sectors such as housing, the hospital, the asylum, the laboratory, the university, family and sexual relations. He refers to these people as 'specific' intellectuals. They do not formulate the global systematic theory which holds everything in place, but analyse the specificity of mechanisms of power. He writes: 'The project, tactics, and goals to be adopted are a matter for those who do the fighting. What the intellectual can do is to provide instruments of analysis, and at present this is the historian's essential role.'[27]

Foucault thinks that many people are obsessed with a determination to make a science out of Marxism. He is particularly critical of those Marxists who say, 'Marxism, as the science of sciences, can provide the theory of science and draw the boundary between science and ideology.'[28] To those who are trying to establish the scientificity of Marxism he asks, 'What types of knowledge do you want to disqualify in the very instant of your demand: "Is it a science?"'[29] In his view the method of genealogy involves a painstaking rediscovery of struggles, an attack on the tyranny of what he calls 'totalizing discourses' and a rediscovery of fragmented, subjugated, local and specific knowledge. It is directed against great truths and grand theories. But he provides no grounds for distinguishing between different struggles and does not seem to be able to commit himself to a conception of the human good.[30]

SOME CRITICISMS OF FOUCAULT'S WORK

Having outlined some of Foucault's arguments against Marxism, I now want to make some criticisms of his work.

The first criticism is this: Foucault refuses to be committed to a general ontology of history, society or the human subject, or to advance any general theory of power. Many commentators, however, believe that this is precisely his strength; his value lies in *particular* analyses (of the clinic, the asylum, the prison). While there is much that is valuable and insightful in these studies, it must be admitted that Foucault's refusal to deal with epistemological questions means that it is difficult to evaluate them. As he does not present his own methodological protocols we do not know what standards should be used to assess his work.[31] What are the procedures by which one archaeologist of knowledge can confirm or question the analyses of another? If we are to engage seriously with Foucault's writings, considerable theoretical work on his epistemological and ontological protocols will have to be done.

In his writings Foucault often describes a coherent rational strategy, but it is not possible to identify a person who conceived it. It seems to be *a strategy without a subject*. In an interview Foucault was asked who or what it is that co-ordinates the activities of agents. His reply, in my opinion, does not answer the question:

> Take the example of philanthropy in the early nineteenth century: people appear who make it their business to involve themselves in other people's lives, health, nutrition, housing; then, out of this confused set of functions there emerge certain personages, institutions, forms of knowledge: public hygiene, inspectors, social workers, psychologists. And we are now seeing a whole proliferation of different categories of social work.[32]

Consider another example: the strategy for the moralization of the working class. Foucault insists that one cannot say that the bourgeois class (on the level of its ideology or its economic project) invented and forcibly imposed this strategy on the working class.[33] The objective existed and the strategy was developed with ever-growing coherence but without it being necessary to attribute to it a subject.

The Panopticon is Foucault's apt metaphor for the anonymous centralization of power. But what is the principle, force or entity which power crushes or subdues? In other words, what does this modern power operate against? How would a situation change if an operation of power was cancelled? Foucault is vague in his replies to these questions. He has difficulty in defining what this power operates against. It seems that power is almost a metaphysical principle. Power is everywhere: it filters up from below, it is produced at every moment. Now, though he remarks that wherever there is power there is resistance, he offers no grounds for encouraging resistance or struggle. This is partly because he believes that there is no constant human subject in history. History does not reveal the gradual triumph of human rationality, nor does it fulfil an ultimate goal. History is uncontrolled and directionless.

In an interview Foucault was asked: 'Given that there are relations of forces and struggles, the question inevitably arises of who is doing the struggling and against whom?' He replied: 'This is preoccupying me. I'm not sure what the answer is.' The interviewer persisted: 'So who ultimately are the subjects who oppose each other?' Foucault answered:

> This is just a hypothesis, but I would say it's all against all. There aren't immediately given subjects of the struggle, one the proletariat, the other the bourgeoisie. Who fights against whom? We all fight each other. And there is always within each of us something that fights something else.[34]

Underlying Foucault's work there seem to be the following presuppositions: One, social power is omnipotent with respect to the psychic formation of the individual. Two, human individuals exist merely as an embodied nexus to be transformed by the deployment of external causal powers. This ontology is immediately qualified by Foucault. Power, he says, always produces resistance. But the question is, why should it? If power cannot be identified with repression (Foucault insists that it is both productive and regulative), what is the mechanism that generates resistance? Why do people resist? Why do they obey? People obey laws because of external reasons (physical force) or because of internal reasons (ideology). Foucault says that people obey or resist for *many* reasons. This may not seem very helpful, but perhaps his work reminds us that we should avoid easy answers.

When Foucault has been pressed to explain resistance he has been forced back to saying that there is 'something in the social body, in classes, groups, and individuals themselves which in some sense escapes relations of power ... an inverse energy, a discharge ... a plebeian quality or aspect'.[35] It is not surprising that Nicos Poulantzas scorned this attempt to ground resistance in an essentialized, absolutized, externalized spirit of refusal. In short, though the phrase 'wherever there is power there is resistance' is an appealing one, there is no doubt that 'resistance' is really a residual category in Foucault's work. It remains unanalysed.

One useful way of thinking about Foucault has been provided by Poulantzas, who found Foucault helpful *as a theorist of specific techniques of power* and of aspects of the state, but who carefully rejected his more general theoretical project. Poulantzas conceded that Foucault's analysis of normalization and the state's role in shaping corporality was superior to his own. Indeed, there are several interesting parallels between the work of Poulantzas and Foucault.[36] The latter considered that power is immanent in all social relations; Poulantzas also argued that all social relations are relations of power. Both theorists adopt a relational approach to power and explore the links between power and strategies. They also agree that power is productive rather than simply repressive and negative. Another similarity is their interest in 'micro-revolts'. Foucault emphasized that there is a multiplicity of dispersed micro-power relations. Poulantzas, too, was interested in the autonomous role of new social movements but he focused more on the question of how such micro-diversity culminates into the macro-necessity of bourgeois domination.

In spite of these similar interests Poulantzas goes on to make some trenchant criticisms. In his view Foucault neglects to study the modern form of the state and how it is derived from capitalist relations of production. He does not see that all social phenomena always occur in relation to the state and class division. To put this in another way, Foucault disregards the fact that domination has its basis in the

relations of production and exploitation and in the organization of the state.

Foucault exaggerates the importance of disciplinary techniques in the modern state and thus neglects the continued
importance of violence, legal coercion and law in general.
Poulantzas argues that law and the state are each characterized equally by negative and positive features. The law is
not only involved in organizing repression but is also
essential for reproducing consent. Likewise the state is not
only involved in repression and police measures, it is also
active in constituting social relations and winning mass
support.

According to Poulantzas Foucault emphasizes only the
repressive, prohibitive side of law and the positive productive
side of (state) power. In emphasizing the internalized
repression achieved through disciplinary normalization, Foucault ignores the direct role coercion plays in sustaining the
web of disciplinary and ideological mechanisms as well as
the continued importance of overt violence in the state's
activities. On the other hand, some commentators have
remarked that the tacit social theory of *Discipline and
Punish* describes all social relations in terms of power,
domination and subordination and that Foucault neglects
aspects of human sociability, in the family and in civil
society generally, which are based on co-operation and
reciprocity.[37]

Let me now try to summarize the main points. Foucault's
historical analyses of specific institutions focus on the themes
of centralization, increasing efficiency (technical rationality),
and the replacement of overt violence by moralization.
Power in modern societies is essentially orientated towards
the production of regimented, isolated and self-policing
subjects. According to Foucault power is everywhere. The
idea that 'power' is located at, or emanates from, a given
point seems to him to be based on a misguided analysis. In
his view power is not always exercised from above in a
negative or repressive way but is an open cluster of relations.
Power is not an institution, a structure, or a certain force
with which certain people are endowed; it is a name given
to a complex strategic relation in a given society. All social

relations are power relations. But if all social relations are power relations, how do we choose between one society and another?

When Foucault has to answer a question such as this he becomes evasive. Theoretically he has put himself in a situation where he cannot use terms like equality, freedom, justice. These concepts are merely tokens in a game, in an interplay of forces. This is a viewpoint very much like that of Nietzsche (who wrote 'when the oppressed want justice it is just a pretext for the fact that they want power for themselves'). History, according to this view, is an endless play of domination.

I said earlier that Foucault does not conceptualize power in terms of the state or the intentionality of an agent, as a property or a possession, or as purely repressive. His analyses of power employ a conception of power as positive, productive and relational. It has been said that Foucault is trapped within a logical 'impasse'. Given his conception of power, there can be no escape, no locus of opposition or resistance, because *power itself has no specific basis or ground*.[38]

According to Foucault the existence of power relations presupposes forms of resistance. Just as power is present everywhere in the social network, so is resistance; there are a multiplicity of resistances which are constantly shifting and regrouping. Foucault does not say more than this. *The concept of resistance remains undeveloped.*

Additionally, *an analysis of the state is absent from his work*. Foucaldians like Donzelot have deliberately decentred the question of the state. They do not believe that the state is the locus or prime operator of power. To put it in another way, they have suspended assumptions concerning the unity, functionality and importance of the state.

Moreover, Foucault believes that it is no longer feasible to conceptualize relations of power simply in terms of the state, class struggle, relations of production and capitalist exploitation. And so it is not surprising that Foucault *underestimates the significance of social class and class struggle* and *neglects the role of law and physical repression*. He is so concerned with the anonymity of modern forms of administration that he neglects class domination.

Foucault's philosophy is embedded in the historical analyses that have been described. It is rooted in story-telling. Foucault neither claims nor seeks scientific status for his analyses. I refer to the fact that he has said that his histories—which seek to forge connections, establish relationships and transgress the established—are fictions:

> I am well aware that I have never written anything but fictions. I do not mean to say, however, that truth is therefore absent. It seems to me that the possibility exists for fiction to function in truth, for a fictional discourse to induce effects of truth ....[39]

There are different systems or 'regimes' of truth; truth is conventional. Foucault wants to avoid questions of epistemology and so in his work truth plays no part in the transformation of knowledges. Instead he celebrates, like Nietzsche, the perspectivity of knowledge.

Foucault is acutely aware that there are different sorts of knowledge; there is disqualified knowledge, knowledge not only from above but from below. His claim that truth is always relative is not easy to accept. It is because of this position that he cannot say that one historical period or society or theory is better than another. This, of course, raises the question: from what position is Foucault able to write his own descriptions? What is the status of his own theory?

In this chapter I have tried to show that Foucault is especially concerned with how knowledge is enmeshed in disciplinary power. He rejects the traditional liberal view that power interferes with the free formation of truth. For Foucault power is necessary for the production of knowledge and is an inherent feature of all social relationships. I want particularly to stress the fact that Foucault and his many followers, both in France and in this country, have been propagating the view that Marxism is authoritarian and outmoded: '... one must try to think of struggle and its forms, objectives, means and processes in terms of a logic free of the sterilising constraints of the dialectic.'[40] Nietzsche's thought has influenced Foucault so deeply that it is not surprising that he rejects Marx's view of economics, history, politics and method. In the next chapter I will consider the influence of Nietzsche's thought on some of the 'younger generation' of post-structuralist thinkers.

CHAPTER 4

Some currents within post-structuralism

NIETZSCHE CONTRA HEGEL

Many post-structuralist thinkers have been greatly influenced by the philosophy of Nietzsche, with its denunciation of the 'illusion' of truth and static notions of meaning, its belief in the will to power, its affirmation of the Dionysian way of life, and its hostility to egalitarianism. To give only a few examples, Michel Foucault was influenced by Nietzsche's thought in the late 1950s, and he began to be critical of historicism and humanism. Another writer, Jean-François Lyotard, who had been a left-wing militant for a long time, denounced the Soviet Union and turned to Nietzsche's ideas. Jacques Derrida constantly invokes Nietzsche in his writing. Gilles Deleuze, too, has been deeply swayed by Nietzsche. Many writers suggest that Marx sublates Hegel by appropriating the radical form (the dialectical method) and dispensing with the conservative content. Deleuze rejects completely both the form and content of Hegel's philosophy and claims that Nietzsche was the first real critic of Hegel and dialectical thought.

Let us try to see how certain features of Nietzsche's philosophy are being used in the polemic against Hegel and Marx. Nietzsche is often misunderstood; he often speaks of 'war' even when he is evidently thinking of 'strife', of 'power' rather than 'self-perfection', and of the 'Dionysian' rather than the 'classical'. I can see that there is much that is appealing in his thought. In Nietzsche's philosophy, for example, there is a sustained celebration of creativity—all genuine creation is a creation of new values and norms. I think that perhaps we should make a distinction between Nietzsche and Nietzscheanism. To be a Nietzschean is in a sense a contradiction in terms; to be a Nietzschean one must not be Nietzschean.

Nietzsche opposed both the idolatry of the state and political liberalism because he was basically anti-political. He loathed the idea of belonging to any 'party' whatever. Nietzsche objects to the state because it appears to him as the power that intimidates men and women into conformity. However, Nietzsche opposes not only the state but any overestimation of the political. In short, the leitmotiv of his life and thought is *the anti-political individual who seeks self-perfection* far from the modern world. He thus thinks that the Goethean man embodies the great contemplative type who is essentially unrevolutionary, even anti-revolutionary.

Nietzsche had strong philosophical reasons for not having a system. He held that a system is reducible to a set of premises which cannot be questioned within the framework of the system: 'The will to a system is a lack of integrity.' All assumptions have to be questioned. No one system reveals the entire truth; at best each adopts one point of view or perspective. We must consider many perspectives and not imprison our thought in one system. Nietzsche held that the coherence of a finite system could never be a guarantee of its truth. His entire attack on systems is based on his objection to the irrationality which he finds in the failure to question premises. For him science is not a finished and impersonal system but a passionate quest for knowledge, an unceasing series of small, courageous experiments. He has in mind the 'gay science' of fearless experiment and the goodwill to accept new evidence and to abandon previous positions if necessary.

There are many important differences between the philosophies of Hegel and Nietzsche. In Hegel's dialectic, concepts are inadequate and contradictions lead to a more adequate concept at a higher level. This process continually repeats itself as the dialectic moves towards the Absolute. In Nietzsche, however, the dialectic undercuts, undermines itself. Hegel always stressed the result of the process, the synthesis, and the larger unit, while Nietzsche concerned himself with the negative and the individual. A consequence of Nietzsche's emphasis on the negative may be seen in the tremendous importance he attached to suffering and cruelty—the negative aspect of self-overcoming. Nietzsche was much concerned with the individual and his/her attempts at self-realization. He was, unlike Hegel, more of a psychologist than a historian. In the end, Nietzsche's emphasis on individuality led him to the conception of a vast plurality of individual wills to power. He asserted that not all people are equally capable of being good and creating the beautiful. It seems that some people are more favoured by nature than others. This is the basis of his opposition to socialism and democracy.

I turn now to a crucial point in Nietzsche's philosophy of history and theory of values. One of his hypotheses was the doctrine of the eternal recurrence. It refers to the unconditional and infinitely repeated circular course of all things. This conception depends on Nietzsche's denial of definite progress, of a plan or goal to give meaning to history or life. He deprecated any faith that pins its hopes on the future. Empirical facts do not seem to him to warrant the belief that history is a story of progress: 'The goal of humanity cannot lie at the end of time but only in its highest specimens' (*Thoughts out of Season*).

In contrast to this view Hegel believed that there was an Absolute Spirit that was working itself through all the concrete manifestations of the world. He held that reality unfolded itself through its contradictions and rose to ever higher levels until Spirit at last became conscious of itself. For all its philosophical idealism this view compels one to see human culture and history as a part of a total process. This is why political institutions, works of art and social customs so often appear as the varied expression of a single inner essence.

Marx abolished the idealism of Hegel's system and stressed the material laws of historical development. He replaced Spirit with Economy; in his view economic forces determined the particular system of social relations that characterizes each stage of historical development. Class struggle became the central principle of historical development.

One of the reasons why I have given the above outline is that many thinkers are opposed to this sort of 'teleological' Marxism. The French right-wing 'new philosophers' assert that Marxism of this sort transforms Marx into the teller of a salvational story rather than a scientific theorist of historical laws. But they say more than this—they contend that there is a direct line from Hegel to the Gulag. The stages are these: first of all there is Hegel's invention of the notion of Absolute Spirit with its teleology of history. Then Marx relocates this teleology within history conceived in materialist terms. Finally, the annulment of contradiction at the end of the teleological process becomes (with Stalinism) an abolition of differences through sheer force. The Absolute Spirit becomes the knock at the door, in the name of history, of the secret police.

DELEUZE AND GUATTARI: THE RETURN TO THE IMAGINARY

One source of the ideas mentioned above is the book *Anti-Oedipus: Capitalism and Schizophrenia*.[1] Its authors, Gilles Deleuze and Félix Guattari, have combined the three concepts 'desire', 'production' and 'machine' from Freud and Marx into a new idea: we are desiring machines. They call the outward, linguistic manifestation of desire *délire*. *Délire* is an effect produced by the machinery of desire. *Anti-Oedipus* stresses the collective nature of *délire* (even if it is produced by an individual) and its social character. At the present time the dominant tendency is to privatize *délire*. Against this trend Deleuze and Guattari have implicitly adopted one of the slogans of the French Left of the 1970s: the personal is the political. There is no separation between the personal and the social, the individual and the collective. Both the political and the psychological field are permeated by the same form of energy, libido, which has effects both political (the class struggle) and individual (*délire*). Libido and politics interpenetrate.

Deleuze and Guattari distinguish two types of desire, the paranoid and the schizophrenic, corresponding to two main forms of society: the fascist and the revolutionary. In social terms, the contrast is between authoritarian and libertarian organizations: on the one hand there are states with their insistence on centralized power; on the other hand looser organizations of smaller groups—imagine a society of nomads—without territorial limits or a system of hierarchy. The authors assert that there are two poles to *délire*: the real *délire* of schizophrenia, centred on flight, and the reactionary *délire* of paranoia based on the authoritarian structure of the hierarchical state.

Politically Deleuze and Guattari are against the process of generalization by which a class is elevated into an abstraction above its members and the party becomes representative of a class. In contrast they believe that revolutionary desire flows through small groups and produces collective action. In other words, it is not enough to fight fascism in the street; we must also fight it in our own heads, setting our revolutionary schizophrenia against our own fascist paranoia. Influenced by the ideas of Wilhelm Reich's *Mass Psychology of Fascism*, they believe that the unconscious is a political force and that fascism dwells in it as much as on the historical stage or in political parties.

The authors of *Anti-Oedipus* argue that Freudian psychoanalysis is an example of 'interpretation as impoverishment'. It is what happens when the lived complexity of a patient's life is 'rewritten' within the confined limits of the Freudian 'family romance'. They go on to attack the reductiveness of all schemes that seek to limit and thus impoverish a complex reality in the name of interpretation. Complex reality is always rewritten in terms of a 'mastercode' or 'master narrative' which is then given as the 'meaning' of what is interpreted. Marxism is one such 'mastercode'. In teleological Marxism there is a providential or salvational account of history as a 'master narrative'.

In a sense, Deleuze and Guattari perceive all explanation or interpretation as an expression of the Nietzschean will to power. But they insist that their attack is not directed against interpretation as such but against Marxism as a 'transcendent' interpretation. *Transcendent interpretation* is transcendent in the sense that its significance is based on going outside the text, on some extratextual set of norms. Against this notion of transcendent interpretation they counterpose their demand for *immanent interpretation*, a mode of analysis that respects the internal norms and values and the complexity as it is given of the reality to be interpreted.

Not only Deleuze and Guattari but also Foucault and the 'new philosophers' have argued that traditional Marxism has been 'transcendent' in the sense that it has produced 'meaning' by allegorizing in terms of the 'mastercode' provided by Marx. They all see in Marxism a prime example of an interpretative system that inevitably transforms itself into an instrument of political and physical domination.

I mentioned just now that Deleuze and Guattari are anti-Freudian. Their arguments against the Oedipus complex are these: since the Oedipus complex is supposed to be universal, the results of any interpretation are known in advance. Freud was just a clairvoyant; he recognized the predictable character of his interpretations. Secondly, the richness of the patient's productions is reduced to ready-made explanations. Hence, Freudian interpretation is a form of repression. Thirdly, there is a patriarchal bias in the Oedipus complex (the reduction of desire to the male sexual organs). These arguments are part of a more general criticism of psychoanalysis. Psychoanalysis imposes Lack, Culture and Law on the unconscious, thus structuring, reducing and repressing desire. The unconscious, on the other hand, is productive; it produces desire and threatens to smother the body politic with it; hence its revolutionary character and the necessity for its repression by psychoanalysis, the watch-dog of the modern state.

Psychoanalysis, it is argued, is basically an interpretation-machine. It translates all the patient says into another language and thus turns the patient into a subject in both senses of the term. Moreover, psychoanalysis depends upon a form of power: the patient submits to the analyst and his flow of libido is reduced to words and interpretations.

An important current within post-structuralism explores the possibilities and potentialities of *desire*. For Deleuze and Guattari desire emerges as a mysterious and disruptive, all-pervading, productive force of libido. The authors idealize Lacan's concept of the imaginary (the stage before the acquisition of language) and emphasize his theory of desire. They see the transition into the symbolic (language, structure and society) as a loss. Entrance into structure and society is seen as a tragedy. Only a return to the imaginary can spell the end of socio-political repression, of the dictatorship of the symbolic. For Deleuze and Guattari the really important condition is schizophrenia. Indeed, attacking classical psycho-analysis and Marxism, they develop a new theory, provoca-tively named schizoanalysis.

Deleuze and Guattari envisage a politics of the Lacanian imaginary. The goal of politics is to return to humankind's freedom, to a sense of being a passionate animal. They glorify the pre-symbolic stage of direct, fusional relationships, of spontaneity, of primitive, unmediated desire. They reject phallocentrism and denounce the family as the bearer of hierarchy and taboo. They look to children, primitive peoples and, most of all, to the mad as examples of people in touch with the power of the pre-symbolic. What these marginal groups are assumed to have in common is that they have not yet been fully 'oedipalized', that is, that the symbolic has not yet entered them. The book is a diatribe against oedipalization. Although the authors' attack on oedip-alization is also an attack on psychoanalysis, the book relies on Lacan's particular way of theorizing the Oedipus complex as the process by which society enters the indivi-dual.

Psychiatric theory is usually based on a negative concept of madness, in which madness is perceived as a deficit, a lack of rationality, a state of being less than one could be. Lacan has never supported this pejorative view. He has spoken of the analyst as someone deeply in touch with the knowledge 'that it is possible for each of us to go mad'. Man's being, he says, cannot be understood without reference to madness, nor would man be man without his carrying madness within as the limit of his freedom. Lacan, then, is sympathetic to the anti-psychiatrists who identify themselves with the mad in so far as they claim to have a message that cannot be communicated in ordinary ways. Like the schizophrenic they have to destroy ordinary language in order to communicate. In the case of anti-psychiatry Lacan's support comes from the way he demolishes the notion that there is a 'normal' self that is autonomous, coherent, its own 'centre'. The notion of the decentred subject is a crucial link between Lacan and the anti-psychiatric movement, which refuses to view madness as something alien to 'normals'.

Deleuze and Guattari are sympathetic to madness. They argue in *Anti-Oedipus* that in modern life there is an incompatibility between reason and impulse—spontaneity is being squeezed out. The authors take Lacan's ideas about the decentred subject and carry them several steps further than he does. They believe that the schizophrenic makes no separation between personal and social experience; his or her personal expressions are themselves political expressions. For the schizophrenic, word and thing are one, saying is doing. The relationship between word and action, wish and action, is direct and immediate. In a way, Deleuze and Guattari advance 'a politics of schizophrenia'. They regard schizophrenia as a privileging experience and believe that the schizophrenic is not trapped within the oedipal prison, in which the complexity and fluidity of the unconscious are distorted, frozen and flattened, but that he is in touch with fundamental truths about society. In short, they exalt the schizophrenic's proximity to the imaginary, to fusional relationships and to flux. The self is all flux and fragmentation, collection of machine parts. In human relationships one whole person never relates to another whole person because there is no such thing as the 'whole person'. There are only connections between 'desiring machines'. Fragmentation is a universal of the human condition, not something specifc to the schizophrenic.

It will not have escaped notice that the work of Deleuze and Guattari proceeds through conceptual dichotomies: the hierarchical state and the nomadic tribe, paranoia and schizophrenia. It is often said that desire differs from need in that it cannot attain fulfilment; it is an ever-renewed failure, a constant yearning. But there are several ways of conceiving desire. In the Lacanian psychoanalytic tradition, for example, it is a striving after a lost primary object. Deleuze and Guattari, however, reject the Lacanian definition of the real as the impossible. They invert it: 'in reality everything becomes possible.' Reality is what my desire fabricates.

Deleuze and Guattari are Nietzschean in the sense that their book is a celebration of 'the numinous energies of existence in a joyous activity of free play'. The schizo

> produces himself as a free man, irresponsible, solitary, and joyous, finally able to say and do something simple in his own name, without asking permission; a desire lacking nothing, a flux that overcomes barriers and codes, a name that no longer designates any ego whatever. He has simply ceased being afraid of becoming mad.[2]

In criticism of Deleuze and Guattari I would argue that their conception of desire culminates in sheer idealism. As a sympathetic commentator on *Anti-Oedipus* has remarked:

> The advice is let yourself go. Do your own thing, scream your own screams. In other words, take risks and go against the grain of common sense. This thesis offers no objective assessment of a state of affairs; it is rather a call for action.[3]

Their notion of productive desire is none other than the Nietzschean will to power. In their view there is only one class, that of the slaves, in which some dominate the others. One consequence of all this is that the class struggle is politely consigned to the museum. Though the vocabulary of *Anti-Oedipus* is sometimes Marxist, sometimes Freudian, the main critical strand is Nietzschean from start to finish.[4]

PRISONERS OF DISCOURSE

In one of its developments post-structuralism became a convenient way of evading political questions altogether. The work of Derrida and others had cast great doubt upon the classical notions of truth, reality, meaning and knowledge. If meaning, the signified, was a passing product of words or signifiers, always shifting and unstable, part-present and part-absent, how could there be any determinant truth or meaning at all? If reality was constructed by our discourse rather than reflected by it, how could we ever know reality itself, rather than merely knowing our own discourse? According to this dogma we can never know anything at all; we are the prisoners of our discourse.

One of Foucault's main concerns is the transition from the classical age to nineteenth-century culture. In all of his works there is a similar narrative framework: the relatively open and freewheeling world of the sixteenth century gives way to the classical age, which is superseded by the densely regulated, 'disciplined' society of today. Serious thinking about modern life has polarized into two sterile antitheses which Marshall Berman has called 'modernolatry' and 'cultural despair'.[5] For the practitioners of the former, from Marinetti and Mayakovsky to Le Corbusier, all the personal and social dissonances of modern life can be resolved by technological and administrative means. The means are all at hand, and the only thing needful is leaders with the will to use them. For the intellectuals of cultural despair, from Eliot and Ezra Pound to Marcuse and Foucault, all of modern life seems uniformly hollow, sterile, flat, 'one-dimensional', empty of human possibilities. Anything that looks or feels like freedom or beauty is really only a screen for more profound enslavement and horror.

There is no freedom in Foucault's world, nor does he have a theory of emancipation. The more powerful the vision of some increasingly total system or logic, the more powerless the reader comes to feel. The critical capacity of Foucault's work is paralysed because the reader is made to think that the project of social transformation is vain, trivial, hopeless. I think Habermas is correct when he argues that Foucault's later work 'replaced' the model of repression and emancipation developed by Marx and Freud with a pluralism of power/discourse formations. 'These formations intersect and succeed one another and can be differentiated according to their style and intensity. They cannot, however, be judged in terms of validity.'[6]

It is largely because of the impact of Foucaldian discourse that many intellectuals feel that they cannot use general concepts any more; they are taboo. The system as a whole cannot be combated because there is in fact no 'system as a whole'. Nor is there any central power; power is everywhere.[7] The only forms of political action now felt to be acceptable are of a local, diffused, strategic kind. The worst error is to believe that such local projects should be brought together.

I want to argue that some of the Nietzschean themes in Foucault's thought are the basis of his anti-Marxist position. He insists that any general theory should be renounced and that life cannot be grasped from a single perspective. Believing that truth and power are linked, he adopts a relativist position; modern society is not necessarily better than past ones. We are not progressing from the dark to the light. Foucault attacks Marxists because they believe that they have deciphered the secret of history. For him history is discontinuous and Marxism is a global totalitarian theory which is out of date.

THE CELEBRATION OF INTENSITY

One can also see the shift away from Marxism if one looks at the political trajectory of Jean-François Lyotard. He was a militant for fifteen years in a small left-wing group called *Socialisme ou Barbarie*. This group, which contained well-known theorists such as Cornelius Castoriadis and Claude Lefort, came out of Trotskyism and developed a critique of Soviet bureaucracy.[8] It argued that both the US and the Soviet Union were state capitalist countries.

Lyotard's first book was a monograph on phenomenology, and traces of this commitment are still very apparent in his work. He has never accepted all the injunctions of structuralism and has criticized aspects of the work of Lévi-Strauss. During the events of 1968 Lyotard was a professor of philosophy at Vincennes. He has written that the preoccupations of *Socialisme ou Barbarie* were expressed in '68; in many ways the student revolt was libertarian and anarchist rather than Marxist. One has only to look at the posters and the graffiti ('it is forbidden to forbid') to realize that the movement was largely a protest against bureaucratization, depersonalization, routinization, repression, and not wholly an expression of class antagonism. In Lyotard's view people began to feel that there was a discrepancy between the rhetoric of Marxism and the actual content of the students' movement. 1968 was the year many people turned away from Marxism.

Lyotard next wrote about the tension between the discursive and the figural (the verbal and the visual) in his book *Discours/figure*.[9] He has always been fascinated by the non-linguistic, is critical of Lacan's view that the unconscious is structured like a language and suggests that it is the Other of language. He associates the unconscious with figural representation and the preconscious with language. Language is on the side of censorship and repression; figural representation is on the side of desire and transgression. Lyotard thinks of modern art as being fragmented and believes that it is liberatory. Fragmentation and disruption are attempts to make the unconscious process visible. Art, then, involves the disruption of convention; but this raises the question, 'Can art exist for ever as a transgression of previous assumptions?'

During the time of *Discours/figure* Lyotard was still writing from within the Marxist tradition, but he was beginning to be critical of some aspects of it. He argued against the Hegelian notion that there is a coincidence between the movement of thought and the movement of reality. He also rejected the Lukácsian view that Marxism is the expression of the revolutionary consciousness of the proletariat, the 'voice of history'.[10] Lyotard argued against this view because he believed that the bureaucratic communist parties often claimed to speak in just such an authoritative (and authoritarian) way. Nevertheless, during this period he wanted to retain the concept of alienation because he was concerned with the individual, unlike Althusser, who rejected it as being an ideological remnant from the work of the young Marx.[11]

In recent years Lyotard has supported symbolic protest actions because he believes that through such actions societal veils are dropped. But it has often been noticed that this sort of activity, an interruption of routine, gradually comes to replace revolutionary political activity itself. Once a political act is severed from revolution and becomes symbolic, then all it does is produce a shock effect, which is also a stylistic device of many artists. In detaching action from political goals this sort of activity becomes a self-defeating convention.

The younger generation of post-structuralist thinkers are very concerned not only with the spontaneous but also with the subjective. Lyotard, for example, values the intensity of experience and suggests that if we are always thinking of what we are, we cannot 'let go'. If we are always theorizing about things, we cannot enjoy them for their own sake. In Lyotard's view there should be a shift from the dominance of dry, abstract thinking to a greater appreciation of the emotional. The main message seems to be that we should move from criticism of the present to hedonistic affirmation. It could be argued against Lyotard that he has forgotten that Nietzsche's affirmative view implies that we have to affirm suffering as well. The importance of Nietzsche is that he tells us to put reason *and* impulse together.

Basically, what the post-structuralists like Lyotard are saying is that there is more to life than politics. If we are totally immersed in the political, we miss what is going on here and now. Marxists are always criticizing the status quo in the name of an ideal. Militants are so inflexible that they have no time to enjoy life as it is now. Ideals cut us off from the present.

Instead of having a nostalgia for an unalienated community that may have existed in the past we should celebrate aspects of contemporary life—its anonymity, its fragmentation, its consumptionism. The post-structuralists also want to extol everything that has been left out in the totalizing theories. And so they focus on the marginal, the excluded. But for how long can a group or movement stress the marginal without becoming marginal itself? Furthermore, it could be argued that if all that matters is intensity (the quest for 'kicks'), then one can get as much intensity acting within the system as outside it.

THE 'NEW PHILOSOPHERS'

Some intellectuals, though not strictly post-structuralists themselves, have been deeply influenced by the post-structuralists and have used their ideas in their attack on Marxism. Ten years after the events of 1968 a group of French intellectuals achieved notoriety by making criticisms of Marxism and the socialist societies. This group, which includes Bernard-Henri Lévy, André Glucksmann, Jean-Marie Benoist and others, made successful use of the media to propagate their views against what they call the dogmatism of Marx, of Marx's logos.

But before I give an exposition of the views of the 'new philosophers', let me enumerate briefly a few of the more common arguments—about the limits and limitations of Marxism—on which their ideas are based. The writings of Marx and Engels clearly express the idea that the economy is determinant in the final instance and that therefore the superstructures are in some sense determined. However, the superstructures are not simply reducible to the economy, they have relative autonomy. One of the most serious consequences of the lack of any precise mechanism connecting these two propositions—economic determination and the relative autonomy of the superstructures—is the absence of a theory of the political level. Additionally, the formal, abstract categories of 'base' and 'superstructure' have become an obstruction to analysis since they have displaced real human activities and historical processes as objects of study.

Moreover, Marx did not produce any coherent or comparative analysis of the political structures of bourgeois class power. There is no developed analysis in his work of the capitalist state.[12] Marx neglected changes in the international state system and did not appreciate the importance of nationalism and national cultures. And what is more, he was a positivist. The positivist conception of science within his works has had harmful consequences for the articulation of a Marxist politics. Indeed, a preoccupation with the scientificity of Marxism is said to be the source of the neglect of the centrality of human agency, experience and consciousness.[13]

There are also problems in Lenin's theory and practice. We are often told that there was a contradiction between his conceptions of workers' councils as a necessary revolutionary form of proletarian power and the subsequent reality of party authoritarianism and the development of a monolithic bureaucratic apparatus.[14] To put it simply, Lenin failed to integrate his doctrine of the party with his account of the soviets.

After Leninism, Stalinism. If it was possible for a single individual to create a personality cult around himself, there must be something wrong with the theory of historical materialism (which denies the role of 'the great individual' in history). On the other hand, if the cult arose from the Soviet system (Lenin?), then socialist society itself must bear the responsibility for the inherent potential of Stalinism.

And then there is the question of socialism. Marxism has little of substance to offer on the nature of the transition from capitalism to socialism. The nature of that which is to emerge from the ruins of bourgeois society remains problematic and relatively unformulated. One of the problems is the difference between the classical vision of Marxism and the reality of actually existing socialism. Marx did not realize that the transitional period of socialism might produce an indissoluble monolithic state machine. It is now quite clear that the power and pervasiveness of the state machine has created a situation in which, even given the abolition of capitalist private property, the producers do not exercise control over the processes of production and distribution, but rather control is centralized, hierarchically organized, and exercised by an élite, ostensibly in the interest of the producers.

Western European countries have seen the apparent decline of a militant working class and the emergence of 'non-class' political–subject groups. During the events of May '68, for example, there arose mass movements, composed of many spontaneously organized 'groupuscles'. There were new social groupings around specific issues such as education, women's liberation, ecology and so forth. The hierarchically organized Marxist parties tended to be conservative and could not represent the interest and desires of the new groups. There were struggles that could not be conceptualized as class struggles. When are Marxists going to learn that the 'political' consists of more than class politics?

Existing socialist societies no longer contribute a good model. The party political organization has become synonymous with the bureaucratic machine. Moreover, powerful and privileged ruling strata have come into being. The various military interventions by the USSR should be considered, as well as the regular violation of human rights in the USSR and other Eastern European states. In short, these societies testify to the limitations of Marxist theory.[15]

The 'new philosophers'' denunciation is largely based on these criticisms. They are fond of comparing the dominance of Marxism in post-war France with the dominance of Aristotle's logic in medieval times. Highly critical of Sartre, they contend that his notion of freedom is irreconcilable with his Marxist views and lean towards the anti-Soviet position adopted by Camus in the early 1950s. The leading publicist of the group, Bernard-Henri Lévy, in his book *La barbarie à visage humain* attacks the Marxist theory of power in which power is seen as maintained by varying combinations of ideological mystification and physical repression.[16] Against this model Lévy deploys a vulgarized fusion of ideas drawn from Foucault and Lacan in which power is everywhere, and yet is 'nothing'. It is nothing since it cannot be located in specific mechanisms of institutions. Rather than being imposed from above it filters up from below, permeating *every* social relation. Now, in Foucault there are at least 'resistances' counterposed to power, but for Lévy there is only the impossibility of liberation: the idea of a good society is an absurd dream.

Besides power, the 'new philosophers' are critical of the concepts of reason, theory and history. The idea that the social formation is an analysable totality is rejected. They seem to have a vision in which conflict is no longer a political conflict between social *classes* but an ethical struggle within the individual between the 'desire for submission' and the 'love of freedom'. In a way, we are all oppressors and we are all oppressed.

The 'new philosophers' see all ideologies which envisage an endpoint to history (historicism) as dangerous and wrong. In their view theories that promise an end to power relations convince people that they can justify present means by that future end and so rationalize labour camps and mass slaughter. Deeply rooted in the unconscious is the lust for power. The only ethical way to live is to take the goal of limiting power as the basis of one's actions without believing that power can ever be eliminated.

It is significant that when Lévy wanted to express this he chose to tell his story through Lacanian concepts. For Lévy a Freudian politics that understands constraint, contradiction and the inevitability of power is our only hope, and it is Lacan who suggests its form with his theory of knots, his new topographical image for the indissociability of the imaginary, symbolic, and real.[17] Power is tied to desire and the impossibility of final resolutions just as the symbolic is tied to the imaginary and the real. There is no escape to the imaginary except through psychosis, and for Lévy this is not a workable solution. There is no Utopia, no 'beach underneath the cobblestones'.

The two writers highly regarded by the 'new philosophers' are Lacan and Foucault. Lacan has never claimed to be a Marxist and has explicitly mocked the idea of 'sexual liberation' in the name of traditional Freudian pessimism. Foucault's work, ever since the beginning, has contained an implicit and explicit critique of Marxist concepts. In many respects Foucault's early book *Madness and Civilization* is privileged above its successors, since it is in this book that the 'new philosophers' find inspiration for their belief in the inherent oppressiveness of reason.

Not only does the new philosophy claim inspiration from his work (as it does from Lacan's) but Foucault himself has in certain respects shared the same intellectual and political trajectory as the militants who have become the 'new philosophers'. On his own account it was the explosion of May '68 and after—the development of localized struggles in the school, the prison, the psychiatric hospital—which made it possible for him to take up explicitly the problem of the interrelation of power and knowledge.[18]

As I remarked earlier, Foucault rejects the traditional conception of power as invested in a central, organizing state from which it filters down to successive levels. To Foucault the state is merely one apparatus amongst many. Both in Foucault and in the 'new philosophers' one comes across the idea that global struggles are recuperative, leading from one domination to another, while only local and partial struggles are truly subversive. It is interesting that several writers have noticed a similarity between Foucault's concept of power, with its rejection of class analysis in favour of a vision of a complex of forces which continually disaggregate and coalesce, and the views of American functionalists.

For the 'new philosophers' socialism is the embodiment of technological rationality and tyranny. Much of their writing is about the concept of Gulag, a term denoting Soviet oppression, derived from Solzhenitsyn. One of their leading representatives, André Glucksmann, has said:

> I reproach Marx with having traced a certain number of intellectual routes: the cult of the total and final Revolution; of the State that terrorizes for the good of the collectivity, and of social science that permits the masses to be guided in spite of themselves. These paths do not lead directly to the Gulag but to non-resistance to the Gulag.[19]

According to the 'new philosophers' there is now a move from the 'scientific', value-free problematic of structuralism to the problematic of the person and human rights. What is being emphasized now is not human subjectivity but the philosophy of the person. Their argument goes like this:

Marxism is concerned with abstract categories like 'the masses'. We should concern ourselves not with abstractions but with respect for the individual. Besides a universal respect for the human person, 'the otherness of others', there must also be a new respect for other cultures and religions. Marxists do not have any respect for the singularity of the human person, they are tyrants who have only contempt for the individual. Their notion of world revolution is a dream, a dangerous fantasy; those who have this dream are terrorists, orphans of violence. Platonists, Leibnizians are not guilty of putting people into concentration camps— Marxists are. Marxism-Leninism leads to the justification of tyranny. The Helsinki Agreement, a legal text signed by East and West, is being broken by the Soviet Union, where many dissidents are being persecuted. We must name those—like Andrei Sakharov— that are incarcerated. The question of human rights has become vital and has made the work of Kant relevant again. His *Critique of Practical Reason* provides a framework within which we can seriously think of ethical problems. Kant insisted that we should treat people not as means but as ends in themselves: 'Always act on that maxim which you can at the same time will to become a universal law.' We must oppose Marxism-Leninism with an ethic of love—love addressed to a single person.[20]

What criticism can be made of such bitter enemies of Hegel, Marx and Lenin? I will be brief. One, the 'new philosophers' criticize only the Soviet Union, never the United States. Two, they never refer to the exploitation and violence of capitalism and its support of authoritarian regimes throughout the world. Three, they are so involved in their 'ethical' concerns that they do not make any attempt to make the world better through political action. In other words, they focus only on the individual and neglect the collective. From listening to some of them I get the impression that the imprisonment of dissidents is the crucial issue. They do not focus on questions such as the danger of nuclear war and the urgent need for a powerful peace movement. Most of the 'new philosophers', who draw heavily on Nietzsche's thought, now reject both science and politics. There is a revival of interest in plurality and difference, the singular and the subjective; and some of them are seeking solace in aesthetics, metaphysics and religion.[21]

CONCLUSION

In this chapter it has been argued that many of the fundamental beliefs of post-structuralism have their roots in Nietzscheanism. If one looks at the work of the post-structuralists, such as Deleuze and Guattari, Derrida, Foucault, Lyotard and others, one can see the influence of Nietzsche's philosophy. They share with him an antipathy to any 'system'. Secondly, they reject the Hegelian view of history as progress. Thirdly, they are aware of the increasing pressure towards conformity and are highly critical of this tendency. Fourthly, their obsession with the subjective and the 'small story' has led them to affirm the anti-political individual.

Post-structuralism is largely 'a product of 1968'. Unable to break the structures of state power, post-structuralism found it possible to subvert the structures of language: 'The student movement was flushed off the streets and driven underground into discourse.'[22] Its enemies became coherent belief-systems of any kind, in particular all forms of political theory and organization which sought to analyse and act upon the structures of society as a whole. All total, systematic thought was now suspect: conceptual meaning itself, as opposed to libidinal gesture and anarchist spontaneity, was feared as repressive.

After briefly introducing the leading post-structuralists I turned to the work of the 'new philosophers'. It was stated that the 'new philosophy' is not just an aberration of a few intellectuals but must be seen as mirroring a widespread mood of disorientation among the generation of '68. The 'new philosophers' believe that human society is permanently and inherently oppressive; but domination is no longer conceived of in class terms. They uphold various forms of romanticism and individualism. They denounce 'science' and any totalizing beliefs in the name of the spontaneous and the particular. Most of these philosophers hold the view that science always operates within and reinforces relations of power; that Marxism is in some way responsible for the terror of the Soviet camps; that the state is the central source

of social and political oppression and that therefore any
politics directed towards the seizure of state power is
dangerous and vain. These ideologues combine an odd
idealization of rebellion with an ultimately passive pessimism
and an acquiescence in the status quo. This is not surprising,
as they have no conception of historical advance or
permanent transformation.

Most of the theorists I have mentioned in this chapter
think of Marxism as the last systematic attempt to understand
the world, to find an immanent order in it. As such, they
argue, it is a metaphysics. Marxism, they assert, no longer
connects with the present. Indeed, it is a belief system which
cuts people off from reality. Lyotard, for example, now sees
Marxism as a form of religious discourse: the suffering
proletariat is supposed to bring about, some time in the
future, the redemption of the world.

The attitude of many post-structuralists seems to be: 'If
Marxism isn't true, then nothing is.' Many thinkers feel that
we are at a stage of confusion ('we don't know where we
are going') and that Nietzsche best expresses that confusion.
The irony is that theorists like Lyotard and others need a
general theory to support their assertion as to why there
cannot be a general theory. As they cannot provide any
grounds for their views, they think of their viewpoint as
being provisional, 'ironic'. Why do these intellectuals focus
only on the heterogeneous, the diverse, the subjective, the
spontaneous, the relative and the fragmentary?

CHAPTER 5

Postmodernism

INTRODUCTION

In the first part of this chapter I will discuss the question of social change in contemporary societies by drawing on the recent work of the French thinker Jean-François Lyotard, whom I briefly introduced in the last chapter. I think that an examination of his thesis can help us to understand some of the main concerns of postmodernism.

I will focus on Lyotard's reflections on science, the changing nature of knowledge in computerized societies, the differences between narrative knowledge and scientific knowledge, the ways in which knowledge is legitimated and sold, and the social changes that may take place in the future.

EDUCATIONAL CHANGE IN COMPUTERIZED SOCIETIES

Many people are aware that Western societies since the Second World War have radically changed their nature in some way. To describe these changes social theorists have used various terms: media society, the society of the spectacle, consumer society, the bureaucratic society of controlled consumption, post-industrial society. A fashionable description of such societies is that they are postmodern. Lyotard is a post-structuralist who adopts a postmodernist stance.

Postmodernism is in part a description of a new type of society but also, in part, a new term for post-structuralism in the arts. (In this chapter I will use postmodernism and post-structuralism synonymously.)

In *The Postmodern Condition* Lyotard argues that during the last forty years the leading sciences and technologies have become increasingly concerned with language: theories of linguistics, problems of communication and cybernetics, computers and their languages, problems of translation, information storage, and data banks.[1]

The technological transformations are having a considerable impact on knowledge. The miniaturization and commercialization of machines is already changing the way in which learning is acquired, classified, made available, and exploited.

Lyotard believes that the nature of knowledge cannot survive unchanged within this context of general transformation. The status of knowledge is altered as societies enter what is known as the postmodern age. He predicts that anything in the constituted body of knowledge that is not translatable into quantities of information will be abandoned and the direction of new research will be dictated by the possibility of its eventual results being translatable into computer language. The old principle that the acquisition of knowledge is indissociable from the training of minds, or even of individuals, is becoming obsolete. Knowledge is already ceasing to be an end in itself. It is and will be produced in order to be sold.

It is widely accepted that computerized knowledge has become the principle *force of production* over the last few decades. This has already had a noticeable effect on the composition of the work-force of the most highly developed countries. (There is a decrease in the number of factory and agricultural workers and an increase in professional, technical and white-collar workers.)[2] Knowledge will be the major component in the world-wide competition for power and it is conceivable that nation-states will one day fight for control of information, just as they battled for control over territories in the past. In the postmodern age science will probably strengthen its pre-eminence in the arsenal of productive capacities of the nation-states and the gap between developed and developing countries will grow even wider.

But already in multinational corporations, which are really new forms of the circulation of capital, investment decisions have passed beyond the control of nation-states. Lyotard suggests that power and knowledge are simply two aspects of the same question: Who decides what knowledge is? Who knows what needs to be decided?[3]

In the computer age the question of knowledge is now more than ever a question of government. It is suggested that the functions of regulation, and therefore of reproduction, are being and will be further withdrawn from administrators and entrusted to machines. Increasingly the central question is: who will have access to the information these machines must have in storage to guarantee that the right decisions are made?

For Lyotard knowledge is a question of competence that goes beyond the simple determination and application of the criterion of truth, extending to the determination of criteria of efficiency (technical qualification), of justice and/ or happiness (ethical wisdom), of beauty (auditory or visual sensibility), etc. Knowledge is what makes someone capable of forming not only 'good' denotative utterances but also 'good' prescriptive and 'good' evaluative utterances. But how are they to be assessed? They are judged to be good if they conform to the relevant criteria (of justice, beauty, truth and efficiency) accepted in the social circle of the 'knower's' interlocutors.

It is important to mention here that Lyotard, who has been greatly influenced by Wittgenstein's notion of language games, makes the following observations.[4] Each of the various categories of utterance can be defined in terms of rules specifying their properties and the uses to which they can be put. The rules of language games do not carry within themselves their own legitimation, but are objects of a contract, explicit or not, between players; if there are no rules, there is no game. Every utterance is thought of as a 'move' in a game. Messages have quite different forms and effects depending on whether they are, for example, denotatives, prescriptions, evaluatives, performatives, etc.[5]

Lyotard believes that language games are incommensurable. He distinguishes the denotative game (in which what is relevant is the true/false distinction) from the prescriptive game (in which the just/unjust distinction pertains) and from the technical game (in which the criterion is the efficient/ inefficient distinction). It seems to me that Lyotard sees language games as essentially embodying a conflictual relationship between tricksters. I said earlier that we always tend to act according to the way in which we conceive of things. One pervasive metaphor in our arguments is war. We say some positions are indefensible, we talk of attacking, demolishing, shooting down other people's arguments. We can win or lose arguments. I maintained in Chapter 4 that we could always use other metaphorical concepts than that of war. For Lyotard, however, to speak is to fight:

> In a discussion between two friends the interlocutors use any available ammunition ... questions, requests, assertions, and narratives are launched pell-mell into battle. The war is not without rules, but the rules allow and encourage the greatest possible flexibility of utterance.[6]

NARRATIVE KNOWLEDGE AND SCIENTIFIC KNOWLEDGE

Scientific knowledge does not represent the totality of knowledge; it has always existed in competition and conflict with another kind of knowledge which Lyotard calls narrative. In traditional societies there is a pre-eminence of the narrative form. Narratives (popular stories, myths, legends and tales) bestow legitimacy upon social institutions, or represent positive or negative models of integration into established institutions. Narratives determine criteria of competence and/or illustrate how they are to be applied. They thus define what has the right to be said and done in the culture in question.

In traditional societies a narrative tradition is also the tradition of the criterion defining a threefold competence—'know-how', 'knowing how to speak' and 'knowing how to hear'—through which the community's relationship to itself and its environment is played out. In the narrative form statements about truth, justice and beauty are often woven together. What is transmitted through these narratives is the set of rules that constitute the social bond.

Lyotard discusses the retreat of the claims of narrative or story-telling knowledge in the face of those of the abstract, denotative or logical and cognitive procedures generally associated with science. In the science language game the sender is supposed to be able to provide proof of what s/he says, and on the other hand s/he is supposed to be able to refute any opposing or contradictory statements concerning the same referent. Scientific rules underlie what nineteenth-century science calls verification, and twentieth-century science falsification.[7] They allow a horizon of consensus to be brought to the debate between partners (the sender and the addressee). Not every consensus is a sign of truth, but it is presumed that the truth of a statement necessarily draws a consensus. Now, scientists need an addressee, a partner who can verify their statements and in turn become the sender. Equals are needed and must be created.

Didactics is what ensures that this reproduction takes place. Its first presupposition is that the student does not know what the sender knows; obviously this is why s/he has something to learn. Its second presupposition is that the student can learn what the sender knows and become an expert whose competence is equal to that of the teacher. As the students improve their skills, experts can confide in them what they do not know but are trying to learn. In this way students are introduced to the game of producing scientific knowledge. In scientific knowledge any already accepted statement can always be challenged. Any new statement that contradicts a previously approved statement regarding the same referent can be accepted as valid only if it refutes the previous statement.

The main difference between scientific knowledge and narrative knowledge is that scientific knowledge requires that one language game, denotation, be retained and all others be excluded. Both science and non-scientific (narrative) knowledge are equally necessary. Both are composed of sets of statements; the statements are 'moves' made by the players within the framework of generally applicable rules. These rules are specific to each particular kind of knowledge, and the 'moves' judged to be 'good' in one cannot be the same as those judged 'good' in another (unless it happens that way by chance). It is therefore impossible to judge the existence or validity of narrative knowledge on the basis of scientific knowledge or vice versa: the relevant criteria are different.

Lyotard argues that narrative knowledge certifies itself without having recourse to argumentation and proof. Scientists, however, question the validity of narrative statements and conclude that they are never subject to argumentation or proof. Narratives are classified by the scientist as belonging to a different mentality: savage, primitive, underdeveloped, backward, alienated, composed of opinions, customs, authority, prejudice, ignorance, ideology. Narratives are fables, myths, legends fit only for women and children.

Here there is an interesting twist in Lyotard's argument. He says that scientific knowledge cannot know and make known that it is the true knowledge without resorting to the other, narrative kind of knowledge, which from its point of view is no knowledge at all. In short, there is a recurrence of the narrative in the scientific.[8]

The state spends large amounts of money to enable science to pass itself off as an epic. The state's own credibility is based on that epic, which it uses to obtain the public consent its decision-makers need. Science, in other words, is governed by the demand of legitimation. The two myths which have acted as justifications for institutional scientific research—that of the liberation of humanity and that of the speculative unity of all knowledge—are also national myths. The first, political, militant, activist, is the tradition of the French eighteenth century and the French Revolution. The second is the German Hegelian tradition organized around the concept of totality. Lyotard examines these two myths as versions of the narrative of legitimation of knowledge.

The subject of the first of these versions is humanity as the 'hero' of liberty. Lyotard writes: 'All peoples have a right to science. If the social subject is not already the subject of scientific knowledge, it is because that has been forbidden by priests and tyrants. The right to science must be reconquered.' The state resorts to the narrative of freedom every time it assumes direct control over the training of 'the people' under the name of the 'nation', in order to point the people down the path of progress.

Lyotard remarks:

> In Stalinism, the sciences only figure as citations from the metanarrative of the march towards socialism, which is the equivalent of the life of the spirit. But on the other hand Marxism can ... develop into a form of critical knowledge by declaring that socialism is nothing other than the constitution of the autonomous subject and that the only justification for the sciences is if they give the empirical subject (the proletariat) the means to emancipate itself from alienation and repression.[9]

According to Lyotard these (older) master narratives no longer function in contemporary society. He argues that the grand narrative has lost its credibility, regardless of whether it is a speculative narrative or a narrative of emancipation. The decline of the unifying and legitimating power of the grand narratives of speculation and emancipation can be seen as an effect of the blossoming of techniques and technologies since the Second World War, which has shifted emphasis from the *ends* of action to its *means*.

THE MERCANTILIZATION OF KNOWLEDGE

With the Industrial Revolution it was found that a technical apparatus requires an investment; but since it optimizes the efficiency with which the task to which it is applied is carried out, it also optimizes the surplus-value from this improved performance. It is at this moment that science becomes a force of production, a moment in the circulation of capital.

An important aspect of research is the production of

proof. Proof needs to be proven. A scientific observation depends on facts being registered by sense organs. But the range and powers of discrimination are limited. This is where technology comes in. Technical devices follow the principle of optimal performance, maximizing output and minimizing input. Technology is, therefore, a game pertaining not to the true, the just or the beautiful, but to efficiency. A technical 'move' is 'good' when it does better and/or expends less energy than another. Devices that optimize the performance of the human body for the purpose of producing proof require additional money. The game of science becomes the game of the rich, in which whoever is wealthiest has the best chance of being right.[10] It is thus that an equation between wealth, efficiency and truth is established.

To put it in another way, the goal in science is no longer truth, but performativity—that is, the best possible input/output equation. Scientists, technicians and instruments are bought not to find truth, but to augment power. Since performativity increases the ability to produce proof, it also increases the ability to be right; the technical criterion cannot fail to influence the truth criterion.

The shift of attention from ends of action to its means, from truth to performativity, is reflected in present-day educational policy. It has been clear for some time that educational institutions are becoming more functional; the emphasis is on skills rather than ideals. It is probable that in the near future knowledge will no longer be transmitted *en bloc* to young people, once and for all; rather it will be served 'à la carte' to adults as a part of their job retraining and continuing education.

To the extent that learning is translatable into computer language and the traditional teacher is replaceable by memory banks, didactics (teaching) will be entrusted to machines linking traditional memory banks (libraries etc.) and computer data banks to terminals placed at the students' disposal. Lyotard argues that pedagogy would not necessarily suffer. The students would have to learn to use the terminals and the new languages; they would have to be taught what is the relevant memory bank for what needs to be known.

It is only in the context of the grand narratives of

legitimation—the life of the spirit and/or the emancipation of humanity—that the partial replacement of teachers by machines may seem inadequate or even intolerable. Lyotard remarks that it is probable that these narratives are already no longer the principal driving force behind interest in acquiring knowledge. The question now being asked by the student, the state or the university is no longer 'Is it true?' but 'What use is it?' In the context of the mercantilization of knowledge, more often than not this question is equivalent to: 'Is it saleable?' And in the context of power-growth: 'Is it efficient?'

It is clear that education must provide not only for the reproduction of skills but also for their progress. Therefore training must be given in all the procedures that can increase one's ability to connect the fields jealously guarded from one another by the traditional organization of knowledge. What is vitally important for students to have is the capacity to actualize the relevant data for solving a problem here and now, and to organize that data into an efficient strategy. Data banks are the encyclopaedia of tomorrow; they are 'nature' for postmodern men and women. What is important is arranging the data in a new way. This capacity to articulate what used to be separate can be called imagination. It is imagination which allows one either to make a new move (a new argument) within the established rules or to invent new rules, that is to say, a new game.

Lyotard writes that countless scientists have seen their invention of new rules ignored or repressed, sometimes for decades, because that invention too abruptly destabilized the accepted positions, not only in the university and scientific hierarchy but also in the discipline. The more striking the invention, the more likely it is to be denied the minimum consensus, precisely because it changes the rules of the game upon which consensus had been based.[11] Lyotard argues that such behaviour is terrorist. By terror he means the efficiency gained by eliminating, or threatening to eliminate, a player from one's language game. He is silenced or consents, not because he has been refuted but because the other players' ability to participate has been threatened: 'Adapt your aspirations to our ends—or else . . .'

BOURGEOIS ART AND ITS FUNCTION IN SOCIETY

Having give an exposition of Lyotard's book, I want to place his thesis in the context of the controversy about modernism and postmodernism. But before I do that I want to contextualize the controversy. The debate about postmodernism is partly about the arts and so in this section I will say something about the institution of art in bourgeois society and the bitter struggle waged against it in the 1920s by the avant-garde.

The best way I can think of understanding the recent development of art is by a glance at Peter Bürger's *Theory of the Avant-Garde*.[12] Distinguishing between sacral, courtly and bourgeois art, Bürger suggests the following historical typology:

Sacral Art (for example, the art of the High Middle Ages) served as a cult object. It was wholly integrated into the social institution 'religion', and was produced collectively as a craft.

Courtly Art (for example, the art of the court of Louis XIV) served the glory of the prince. It was part of the life-praxis of courtly society, just as sacral art was part of the life-praxis of the faithful. Courtly art is different from sacral art in that the artist produced as an individual and developed a consciousness of the uniqueness of his individuality.

Bourgeois Art. Whereas in different ways both sacral and courtly art are integral to the life-praxis of the recipient, bourgeois art forms a sphere which lies outside the praxis of life.

The tension between art as an institution and the content of individual works tends to disappear in the second half of the nineteenth century. All that which is dissociated from the praxis of life now becomes the content of works of art. The terminal point is reached in aestheticism, a movement in which art becomes the content of art.

Aestheticism, Bürger writes, must be seen in connection with the tendency towards the division of labour in bourgeois

society. Gradually the artist also turns into a specialist. As
the social subsystem 'art' defines itself as a distinct sphere,
the positive aspect is aesthetic experience. Its negative side
is the artist's loss of any social function.

What, then, is the function of art in bourgeois society?
Herbert Marcuse has argued that works of art are not
received as single entities, but within institutional frameworks
and conditions that largely determine the function of the
works.[13] In his seminal essay 'The Affirmative Character of
Culture' Marcuse has described art's function in bourgeois
society as a contradictory one: on the one hand it shows
'forgotten truths' (thus it protests against a reality in which
these truths have no validity), on the other, such truths are
detached from reality. The term 'affirmative' therefore
characterizes the contradictory function of a culture that
retains 'remembrance of what could be', but is simultaneously
a justification of the established form of existence. Through
the enjoyment of art the atrophied bourgeois individual can
experience the self as personality. But because art is detached
from daily life, this experience remains without tangible
effect—it cannot be integrated into that life.

Let me recapitulate Marcuse's argument. All those needs
that cannot be satisfied in everyday life, because the principle
of competition pervades all spheres, can find a home in art,
because art is removed from the praxis of life. Values such
as humanity, joy, truth, solidarity are excluded from life
and preserved in art. In bourgeois society art has a
contradictory role, it projects the image of a better life and
to that extent protests against the bad order that prevails.
But by realizing the image of a better order in *fiction*, which
is semblance only, it neutralizes those forces that make for
change. Marcuse demonstrates that bourgeois culture exiles
humane values to the realm of the imagination and thus
precludes their potential realization. Art thus stabilizes the
very social conditions against which it protests.

As long as art interprets reality or provides satisfaction
of residual needs only in the imagination it is, though
detached from the praxis of life, still related to it. It is only
in aestheticism that the tie to society, still existent up to this
moment, is severed. The term 'the autonomy of art' is used

to describe *the detachment of art* as a special sphere of human activity from the praxis of life. But somehow this concept blocks recognition of the social determinacy of the process. The idea of the relative dissociation of the work of art from the praxis of life in bourgeois society has become transformed into the erroneous idea that the work of art is totally independent of society. We should remember that this detachment of art from practical contexts is a historical process; it is socially conditioned. Perhaps the reason that the artist's product could acquire importance as something special, 'autonomous', lies in the continuation of the handicraft mode of production after the division of labour—and the separation of workers from their means of production—had become the norm.

THE MAIN FEATURES OF THE AVANT-GARDE

Only after art has detached itself completely from the praxis of life can two things be seen: the progressive separation of art from real life contexts and the crystallization of a distinctive sphere of experience—the aesthetic.

Let us now turn to the historic avant-garde and its attempt to negate the autonomy of art.[14] (There may be several avant-gardes; Bürger's term 'the historic avant-garde' refers to the uniqueness of the avant-garde movements of the 1920s such as Dadaism and Surrealism.) The production of the autonomous work of art is generally seen as the act of an individual—who is often a genius. The avant-garde's response to this is *the negation of the category of individual creation*. For example, Marcel Duchamp, by signing mass-produced objects, mocked a society in which the signature meant more than the quality of the work.

The avant-garde did not develop a style; there is no such thing as a Dadaist or Surrealist style. One of the characteristics of the avant-garde is the availability to it of and its mastery over artistic techniques of past epochs. It is through the efforts of the avant-garde that the historical *succession* of techniques and styles has been replaced by a *simultaneity* of the radically disparate. For the Surrealists a general openness to impressions is not enough. They attempt to bring the extraordinary about. In the avant-garde movements *shocking the recipient* becomes the dominant principle of artistic intent. Moreover, the Surrealists emphasize the role of *chance*. Starting from the experience that a society organized on the basis of a means–ends rationality increasingly restricts the individual's scope, the Surrealists attempted to discover elements of the unpredictable in daily life.

The avant-garde is totally opposed to society as it is. Bürger writes:

> Since the Surrealists do not see that a given degree of control over nature requires social organization, they run the risk of expressing their protest against bourgeois society at a level where it becomes protest against sociality as such. It is not the specific object, profit as the governing principle of bourgeois-capitalist society, that is being criticized but means-ends rationality as such. Paradoxically, chance, which subjects man to the totally heteronomous can thus seem a symbol of freedom.[15]

It is with the avant-garde movements that self-criticism begins. The main point is that they no longer criticized schools that preceded them, but criticized *art as an institution*. The avant-garde turns against both the distribution apparatus on which the work of art depends and the status of art in bourgeois society as defined by the concept of autonomy. This protest, whose aim it is to reintegrate art into the praxis of life, reveals the nexus between autonomy and the absence of any consequences—art's lack of social impact.

Of course, we now know that the attack of the historic avant-garde on art as an institution failed.[16] Art as an institution continues to survive. Ironically, the procedures invented by the avant-garde with anti-artistic intent are now being used for artistic ends by the postmodernists.

MODERNISM AND POSTMODERNISM

As I said at the beginning of the chapter, there is a general feeling among many thinkers that at some point after the

Second World War a new kind of society began to emerge. This society is labelled in various ways depending on the way it is analysed: consumer society, post-industrial society, society of the spectacle, postmodernist society, etc. Post-structuralists, on the whole, argue that this new society is post-Marxist. They assert that Marxist theory is now outmoded; it does not and cannot apply to the new social developments. This argument often overlaps with another one concerning modernism and postmodernism. The crucial question in these debates is: Has the Enlightenment project failed? Should we, like the post-structuralists and postmodernists, declare the entire project of modernity a lost cause? Or should we try to hold on to the intentions and aims of the Enlightenment and of cultural modernism?

The project of modernity formulated in the eighteenth century by the philosophers of the Enlightenment consisted in their efforts to develop objective science, universal morality and law and autonomous art. Philosophers like Condorcet wanted to use this accumulation of specialized culture for the enrichment of everyday life. They hoped that the arts and sciences would promote not only the control of natural forces but also understanding of the world and of the self, moral progress, the justice of institutions and even the happiness of human beings.

But what has happened is in marked contrast to the hopes and ideals of the Enlightenment. Gradually each domain has been institutionalized; science, morality and art have become autonomous domains separated from the life-world. The structures of cognitive–instrumental, of moral–practical and of aesthetic–expressive rationality have come under the control of special experts.[17]

In America, France and elsewhere, cultural modernism is now under attack from many different quarters. An American neo-conservative, Daniel Bell, made a powerful critique some years ago of modernity.[18] According to Bell modernist culture had infected the values of everyday life. Because of the forces of modernism the principle of unlimited self-realization, the demand for authentic self-experience and the subjectivism of a hyperstimulated sensitivity have come to be dominant. This unleases hedonistic motives irreconcilable with the discipline of professional life in society. Neo-conservatives like Bell see hedonism, the lack of social identification, the lack of obedience, narcissism, the withdrawal from status and achievement competiton as the result not of successful capitalist modernization of the economy but of cultural modernism.

More recently, the Enlightenment project has been denounced by the French 'new philosophers' and their contemporary English and American counterparts. It has also been attacked, less stridently but with more intellectual sharpness, by the post-structuralists. I believe that their work should be included among the manifestations of postmodernism.

The concept of postmodernism is ambiguous and is not yet widely understood. It has probably emerged as a specific reaction against the established forms of high modernism. For some thinkers postmodernism is a periodizing concept whose function is to correlate the emergence of new features in culture. The concept seems to be connected with the appearance, between the 1950s and the 1960s, of a new social and economic order. Sometimes a useful distinction is made between premodernists, those who want to withdraw to a position anterior to modernity, antimodernists and postmodernists. In my opinion post-structuralists like Foucault, Derrida and Lyotard are postmodernists. There are so many similarities between post-structuralist theories and postmodernist practices that it is difficult to make a clear distinction between them.

THE MAIN FEATURES OF POSTMODERNISM

We may be able to understand postmodernism better by returning to Lyotard and seeing what he means by 'modern'. Lyotard uses the term 'modern'

> to designate any science that legitimates itself with reference to a metadiscourse . . . making an explicit appeal to some grand narrative, such as the dialectics of the Spirit, the hermeneutics of meaning, the emancipation of the rational or working subject or the creation of wealth.[19]

To put it another way:

> Societies which anchor the discourses of truth and justice in the great
> historical and scientific narratives (récits) can be called modern. The
> French Jacobins don't speak like Hegel but the just and the good are
> always found caught up in a great progressive odyssey.[20]

Postmodernists distrust metanarratives; there is a deep
suspicion of Hegel, Marx and any form of universal
philosophy.

For Lyotard, then, the postmodern condition is one in
which the *grands récits* of modernity—the dialectic of Spirit,
the emancipation of the worker, the accumulation of wealth,
the classless society—have all lost credibility.[21] He goes on
to define a discourse as modern when it appeals to one or
another of these *grands récits* for its legitimacy. The *grands
récits* are master narratives—narratives of mastery, of man
seeking his *telos* in the conquest of nature. The Marxist
master narrative ('the collective struggle to wrest a realm of
Freedom from a realm of Necessity') is only one version
among many of a modern narrative of mastery. The advent
of postmodernity signals a crisis in a narrative's legitimizing
function, its ability to compel consensus.

Lyotard is critical of Marxism because he holds that it
wishes to create a homogeneous society which can only be
brought about through the use of coercion. He believes that
the individualistic, fragmented society that we have today is
here to stay. Yet, oddly enough, he seems to be nostalgic
for a premodern (traditional) society. As I said earlier,
traditional societies stress narrative, that is to say, myth,
magic, folk wisdom and other attempts at explanation.[22]
Lyotard believes that there is a conflict between narrative
and science (theoretical knowledge). Narrative is disappear-
ing and there is nothing to replace it. He seems to want the
flexibility of narrative knowledge—in which the aesthetic,
cognitive and moral are interwoven—and yet want also to
retain the individualism which developed with capitalism.

Lyotard argues that art, morality and science (the beautiful,
the good and the true) have become separated and autonomous. A characteristic of our times is the fragmentation
of language games. There is no metalanguage. No one can

grasp what is going on in society as a whole. He seems to be saying that there is no one system of domination. There are parallels between these ideas and some right-wing theorists (like Hayek) who argue that society works much better in terms of micro-events; a society that is left to market forces is better than a consciously planned society.

In short, the argument of Lyotard (and some other post-structuralists) is this: big stories are bad, little stories are good. Instead of a truth/falsity distinction Lyotard adopts a small/grand narrative criterion. Narratives are bad when they become philosophies of history. Grand narratives have become associated with a political programme or party, while little narratives are associated with localized creativity. (The stress on the local has often been associated with the Conservative tradition, with the thinking of Edmund Burke and others.) These ideas are similar to those held by Foucault, who is also against grand narratives and supports the idea of local struggles. But what puzzles me is this: why are the post-structuralists so frightened of the universal? And why is Lyotard telling us yet another grand narrative at the end of grand narrative?

Two significant features of postmodernism, as described by the American critic Fredric Jameson, are 'pastiche' and 'schizophrenia'.[23] Jameson begins by explaining that the great modernisms were predicated on the invention of a personal, private style. The modernist aesthetic was organically linked to the conception of an authentic self and a private identity which can be expected to generate its own unique vision of the world and to forge its own unmistakable style. The post-structuralists argue against this; in their view the concept of the unique individual and the theoretical basis of individualism are ideological. Not only is the bourgeois individual subject a thing of the past, it is also a myth, it never really existed in the first place; it was just a mystification. And so, in a world in which stylistic innovation is no longer possible all that is left, Jameson suggests, is pastiche. The practice of pastiche, the imitation of dead styles, can be seen in the 'nostalgia film'. It seems that we are unable to focus on our present. We have lost our ability to locate ourselves historically. As a society we have become incapable of dealing with time.

Postmodernism has a peculiar notion of time. Jameson explains what he means in terms of Lacan's theory of schizophrenia. The originality of Lacan's thought in this area is to have considered schizophrenia as a language disorder. Schizophrenia emerges from the failure of the infant to enter fully into the realm of speech and language. For Lacan the experience of temporality, human time, past, present, memory, the persistence of personal identity is an effect of language. It is because language has a past and a future, because the sentence moves in time, that we can have what seems to us a concrete or lived experience of time. But since the schizophrenic does not know language articulation in that way, he or she does not have our experience of temporal continuity either, but is condemned to live in a perpetual present with which the various moments of his or her past have little connection and for which there is no future on the horizon. In other words, schizophrenic experience is an experience of isolated, disconnected material signifiers which fail to link up into a coherent sequence.

On the one hand, then, the schizophrenic does have a more intense experience of any given present of the world than we do, since our own present is always part of some larger set of projects which includes the past and the future. On the other hand, the schizophrenic is 'no one', has no personal identity. Moreover, he or she does nothing since to have a project means to be able to commit oneself to a certain continuity over time. The schizophrenic, in short, experiences a fragmentation of time, a series of perpetual presents. Jameson contends that experiences of temporal discontinuity, similar to those described above, are evoked in postmodernist works such as the compositions of John Cage and the texts of Samuel Beckett.

TOTALITY OR FRAGMENTATION

You may have noticed that I have made several references to totality and fragmentation. I have said that Lyotard repudiates the big stories, the metanarratives of Hegel and Marx; he believes that no one can grasp what is going on in a society as a *whole*. It seems fashionable nowadays to say that there is no single theoretical discourse which is going to offer an explanation for all forms of social relations or for every mode of political practice. Postmodernists and others are always making this point against Marxism: they insist that it has totalizing ambitions and resent its claim to provide explanations for all aspects of social experience.

Rejecting totality, Lyotard and other postmodernists stress fragmentation—of language games, of time, of the human subject, of society itself. One of the fascinating things about the rejection of organic unity and the espousal of the fragmentary is that this belief was also held by the historic avant-garde movements. They too wanted the dissolution of unity. In their activities the coherence and autonomy of the work was deliberately called into question or even methodically destroyed.

Walter Benjamin's concept of allegory has been used as an aid to understanding avant-gardiste (non-organic) works of art.[24] Benjamin described how the allegorist pulls an element out of the totality of the life context, isolating it, depriving it of its function. (Allegory is thus essentially a fragment, the opposite of the organic symbol.) Then the allegorist joins several isolated fragments and thereby creates meaning. This is posited meaning and does not derive from the original context of the fragments.

These elements of Benjamin's concept of allegory accord with what is called montage, the fundamental principle of avant-garde art. Montage presupposes fragmentation of reality; it breaks through the appearance of totality and calls attention to the fact that it is made up of reality fragments. The avant-gardiste work proclaims itself an artificial construct, an artefact. The opposite holds true for the organic work: it seeks to make unrecognizable the fact that it has been made. In the organic work of art the material is treated as a whole, while in the avant-gardiste work the material is torn out of the life totality and isolated. The aesthetic avant-gardist fragment *challenges* people to make it an integrated part of their reality and to relate it to their experience. The best example of this principle is probably the Brechtian play. A play by Brecht does not aim at organic unity but consists of interruptions and juxtapositions which disrupt conventional expectations and force the audience into critical speculation.

The question as to whether a work of art should be an organic unity or consist of fragments is perhaps best understood by having a look at the debate between Georg Lukács and Theodor Adorno.[25] The contrast between organic and non-organic work underlies both Lukács' and Adorno's theories of the avant-garde. Whereas Lukács holds onto the organic work of art ('realism') as an aesthetic norm and from that perspective rejects avant-gardiste works as decadent, Adorno elevates avant-gardiste, non-organic work to a historical norm and condemns all efforts to create a realistic art in our time.

While Lukács adopted Hegel's view that the organic work of art (for example, the realistic novels of Goethe, Balzac, Stendhal) constitutes a type of perfection, Adorno believed that the avant-garde work is the only possible authentic expression of the contemporary state of the world, the historically necessary expression of alienation in late capitalist society. Like Adorno, Lukács believed that the work of the avant-garde is the expression of alienation in capitalist society, but he was very scathing about the blindness of bourgeois intellectuals who could not see the real historical counterforces working towards a structural transformation of society.

Adorno, however, did not have this political perspective. He believed that instead of baring the contradictions of society in our time, the organic work promotes, by its very form, the illusion of a world that is whole.[26] For him avant-gardiste art is a radical protest that rejects all false reconciliation with what exists and is therefore the only art form that has historical legitimacy. Lukács, on the other hand, acknowledges its character as protest but condemns avant-gardiste art because that protest remains abstract, without historical perspective and blind to the real counter-forces that are striving to overcome capitalism. He rejects the idea that avant-gardiste work allows ruptures and 'gaps' of reality to show through the fragmentary nature of the work itself.

But an important similarity between Lukács and Adorno should be noted: they both argue within the institution of art and are unable to criticize it as an institution for that very reason. I hope that I have said enough to signal that the Lukács–Adorno debate really consists of two antagonistic theories of culture. Adorno not only sees late capitalism as definitely stabilized but also feels that historical experience has shown the hopes placed in socialism to be ill-founded. In this respect he is very much like most of the postmodernists.

It could be said that there are two main traditions or modes of understanding the avant-garde. The first mode of thought is associated with Adorno, Artaud, Barthes, Breton, and Derrida. (Many writers have pointed out that the philosophies of Derrida and Adorno display interesting similarities.) The other mode of thought is associated with Benjamin and Brecht.

It is largely from the work of Benjamin that we have learnt that the social effect of a work of art cannot simply be gauged by considering the work itself but that it is decisively determined by the institution within which the work functions. It is art as an institution which determines the measure of political effect avant-garde works can have and which determines that art in bourgeois society continues to be a realm distinct from the praxis of life. Art as an institution neutralizes the political content of the individual work. It prevents the contents of work that press for radical change in a society—the abolition of alienation—from having any practical effect. Received in the context of artefacts whose shared characteristic is their apartness from the praxis of life, 'organic' works of art tend to be perceived as 'mere' art products.

It should be remembered that had there never been any avant-garde movements, Brecht's and Benjamin's reflections regarding a restructuring of the production apparatus would not have been possible. Brecht never shared the intention of the historic avant-garde artists to destroy art as an institution. Though he despised the theatre of the educated bourgeoisie, he did not conclude that the theatre should be abolished altogether: instead he proposed to radically change it.[27]

I believe that there are so many difficulties with the positions of Lukács and Adorno that they are both unsatisfactory. I want to suggest that one possible way out of the situation may be through the use of the materialist theories inspired by Benjamin and Brecht. In the next section I will make some critical comments on the Lyotardian neo-conservative position and then move on to present a case for what he rejects, the 'grand narrative' of human emancipation.

SOME CRITICISMS OF LYOTARD'S WORK

Lyotard's book *The Postmodern Condition* is on one level about the status of science and technology, about technocracy and the control of information. But on another level it is a thinly veiled polemic against Jürgen Habermas, who stands for a 'totalizing' and dialectical tradition. Habermas thinks that the totality of life has become splintered and argues that the cognitive, ethical and political discourses should come closer together. He wants, in short, to defend modernity against the neo-conservative postmodernists.

In contrast, Lyotard's main target is the Hegelian-Marxist concept of totality. He is scornful of Habermas's vision of a transparent, fully communicational society and sees language situations as an unstable exchange between speakers, as the 'taking of tricks', the trumping of an adversary. He repudiates, in short, Habermas's notion of a consensus community. Lyotard's view of science and knowledge is that of a search not for consensus but for 'instabilities'; the point is not to reach agreement but to undermine from within the very framework in which the previous 'normal science' had been conducted.

Lyotard thinks that Habermas makes the assumption that it is possible for all speakers to come to agreement on which rules are universally valid for language games, when it is clear that language games are incommensurable, subject to heterogeneous sets of pragmatic rules. He argues that the principle of consensus as a criterion of validation, as elaborated by Habermas, is inadequate: it is a conception based on the validity of the narrative of emancipation.[28] Lyotard writes, 'We no longer have recourse to the grand narrative—we can resort neither to the dialectic of Spirit nor even to the emancipation of humanity as a validation for postmodern scientific discourse.'[29] In his view the little narrative (petit récit) remains the quintessential form of imaginative invention.

Influenced by Nietzsche, post-structuralists like Lyotard attack philosophy as an imposition of truth. (Nietzsche is famous for his attack on truth; all perspectives, he said, are illusory.) At one time Lyotard supported Marxism but he now sees it as one of the 'grand narratives' he is against. He writes about the force of language beyond truth and wants to develop a theory of philosophical fiction—a discourse that tries to persuade without the traditional notion of 'argument'. In Lyotard's work problems of power are put to one side, and his views have led him to a form of relativism.

There is an ambiguity throughout Lyotard's work and that of other post-structuralists who have been influenced by Nietzsche's critique of systems. Lyotard argues that all theoretical conceptualizations, such as history, are coercive; in his view any interpretation of history is dogmatic. He does not make a distinction between large-scale theories and dogmatism; it is taken for granted that any large-scale theory is dogmatic. Now, it could be argued that some Marxist theories are dogmatic but that, given time and effort, the dogmatism could be dissolved. However, the post-structuralists never consider this possibility.

Why is this? Richard Rorty has suggested an explanation. He has criticized writers like Foucault and Lyotard for their extraordinary *dryness*:

> It is a dryness produced by a lack of identification with any social context, any communication. Foucault once said that he would like to write 'so as to have no face'. He forbids himself the tone of the liberal sort of thinker who says to his fellow citizens: '*We* know that there must be a better way to do things than this; let us look for it together.' There is no 'we' to be found in Foucault's writing, nor in

those of many of his French contemporaries .... It is as if thinkers
like Foucault and Lyotard are so afraid of being caught up in one
more metanarrative about the fortunes of 'the subject' that they cannot
bring themselves to say 'we' long enough to identify with the culture
of the generation to which they belong.[30]

Politically, it is clear that thinkers like Lyotard and Foucault
are neo-conservatives. They take away the dynamic which
liberal social thought has traditionally relied upon. They
offer us no theoretical reason to move in one social direction
rather than another. On the whole, post-structuralists think
of rationality as a limiting framework. They are against what
they call the imperialism of reason. Lyotard's intellectual
trajectory has brought him to the position where he now
wants to abstain from anything that is connected with the
'metanarrative of emancipation'.

Conclusion

TAKING HISTORY SERIOUSLY

Lyotard is only one of many post-structuralists, 'new philosophers' and others who attack Marxism for being a 'grand narrative' and mock its belief in the emancipation of humanity. As they assert that Marx's story under Hegel's inspiration clearly exhibits a providential plot, it is important to ask, 'What is "narrative"?' One of the insights of recent literary theory is that narrative or story is not specifically a literary form. Fredric Jameson believes that narrative is really not so much a literary form or structure as an epistemological category.[1] Like the Kantian concepts of space and time, narrative may be taken not as a feature of our experience but as one of the abstract or 'empty' co-ordinates within which we come to know the world, a contentless form that our perception imposes on the raw flux of reality. This is not to say that we make up stories about the world to understand it; Jameson is making the much more radical claim that the world comes to us in the shape of stories.

Jameson argues that it is hard to think of the world as it would exist outside narrative. Anything we try to substitute for a story is, on closer examination, likely to be another sort of story. Physicists, for example, 'tell stories' about subatomic particles. Anything that presents itself as existing outside the boundaries of some story (a structure, a form, a category) can only do so through a kind of fiction. In Jameson's view structures may be abundantly useful as conceptual fictions, but reality comes to us in the form of its stories. Narrative, just by being narrative, always demands interpretation, and so we must always be aware of the distinction between manifest meaning and latent content. Moreover, we should remember that every narrative simultaneously presents and represents a world, that is, simultaneously creates or makes up a reality and asserts that it stands independent of that same reality. In other words, narrative seems at once to reveal or illuminate a world and to hide or distort it.

Narrative, the contentless form of our most basic experience of reality, has a function: it is a specific mechanism through which the collective consciousness represses historical contradictions. This is what is meant by 'the political unconscious'. Ironically, it was Freud who actually discovered the political unconscious but who, imprisoned through ideological circumstance within such illusory categories as 'the individual psyche' and the like, was in no position to understand the consequences of his discovery.

It is obvious that Jameson has been much influenced by structuralist thinking: there is the idea, for example, that the notion of 'individual consciousness' is incoherent. (This notion, he would say, implies some idea of a 'collective consciousness' or total social system.) For Jameson Marxism is the story of a fall out of collective life and consciousness into a world of estrangement and alienation where 'individual identity' becomes a primary category within thought. He would say that separation or individuality at the level of consciousness is itself a symptom of estrangement from the life of the collective. To treat the 'I', the feeling or experience of individual identity, as the main ontological category is to repress history itself.

Jameson is antagonistic to those post-structuralists who reject the idea of a master code or master narrative. He finds the notion of master code a valuable one and uses it in his own work. He argues that formalism, whose claims are based on immanent interpretation, is really a form of transcendent interpretation in disguise. Formalist criticism simply rewrites literary works in terms of an ethical master code that is a product of its historical moment. Another example is structuralism, a form of transcendent interpretation that uses the master code language.

Jameson argues that the 'master code' of any interpretative method is the ideology it works to perpetuate. Ideology is the repression of those underlying contradictions that have their source in history. Jameson conceives of ideologies as strategies of containment, and of literature as an ideological production mirroring such strategies at the level of individual works.[2] He tries to subject literature to symptomatic analysis, a mode of interpretation that reveals the specific ways in which works deny or repress history. Symptomatic analysis is also able to show that critical approaches usually assumed to be in competition with one another (the Freudian, the formalist, the structuralist, etc.) share at the deep level an identical set of assumptions, they deny history in an identical way.[3] This method has some similarities with Foucaldian or Nietzschean 'genealogy', which elicits from the structure of a cultural text that unexpressed subtext or *hors texte* it cannot acknowledge. What Jameson tries to do is to find certain patterns which represent strategies of containment; he looks at gaps or absences as specific signs of the way the text denies or represses history.

In Jameson's view taking history seriously means accepting some story as the means of knowing anything at all. (Indeed, I would argue that the more people believe that history should be moving towards the establishment of a rational society, the more likely history will be moving towards it. By making this link between theory and practice we make history conform to our notion of it.) Jameson defends the concept of 'mode of production'; the 'story' of the successive modes of production is heuristic and the value of the concept lies in its use as an instrument of social analysis. What the concept 'mode of production' is really concerned with is not some story of successive economic stages but the possibility of seeing all the social phenomena within a given historical framework as related to one another as to a totality.

Jameson conceives the social totality as something always constituted by a class struggle between a dominant and a labouring class, and he wants us to think of the social order at the cultural level in the form of a dialogue between *antagonistic class discourses*. This dialogue is always made possible by what he calls the unity of a shared code. (It is easy to forget that disagreement is made possible only by a shared language and a common set of assumptions.) The example Jameson provides is that of England in the 1640s when religion operated as the shared code within which was fought out the antagonism between opposing discourses. Historically speaking, we 'hear' only one voice because a hegemonic ideology suppresses all antagonistic class voices, and yet the hegemonic discourse remains locked into a dialogue with the discourse it has suppressed.

TOWARDS A PEDAGOGICAL POLITICAL CULTURE

The controversy over postmodernism is one example of class struggle at the cultural and political level. On the political level postmodernism is an attack on Marxism. On the cultural level it is a repudiation of the modern movement: abstract expressionism in painting, the international style in architecture, existentialism in philosophy. Most postmodernists reject the following models: the existential model of authenticity and inauthenticity, the semiotic opposition between signifier and signified, the Freudian model of latent and manifest, and the Marxist one of appearance and essence (the view that the empirical world, 'appearance', is causally connected to deeper levels, the structures and processes of the real, 'the essence'). These 'depth' models have been replaced by a conception of practices, discourses and textual play.

Jameson suggests that with postmodernism there has emerged a new kind of flatness or depthlessness, a new kind of superficiality.[4] The shift from the period of modernism to the world of the postmodern can be characterized as one in which the alienation of the subject is displaced by *the fragmentation of the subject*. The disappearance of the individual subject and the unavailability of unique and personal style has brought about a new practice: pastiche.

To recapitulate, pastiche has become a ubiquitous mode (in film, especially) which suggests that we wish to be recalled to times less problematic than our own. There seems to be a refusal to engage with the present or to think historically, a refusal that Jameson regards as characteristic of the 'schizophrenia' of consumer society. He believes that there has been a disappearance of a sense of history. Our entire contemporary social system has little by little begun to lose its capacity to retain its own past; it has begun to live in a perpetual present.

There seems to be a random cannibalization of all the styles of the past. At the same time we seem increasingly incapable of fashioning representations of our current experiences. For Jameson postmodernism replicates, reinforces the logic of consumer capitalism. The emergence of postmodernism is closely related to the emergence of present-day multinational capitalism.

Jameson has usefully periodized the stages of realism, modernism and postmodernism by drawing on the work of the economist Ernest Mandel. Mandel, who argues that technology is the result of the development of capital rather than some primal cause in its own right, outlines three fundamental leaps in the evolution of machinery under capital: machine production of steam-driven motors since 1848, machine production of electric and combustion motors since the '90s of the nineteenth century, and machine production of electronic and nuclear-powered apparatuses since the '40s of the twentieth century. This periodization underlines the general thesis of Mandel's book *Late Capitalism*, namely that there have been three fundamental moments in capitalism: market capitalism, monopoly capitalism (or imperialism) and multinational capitalism.[5]

Among the theorists of the New Right the assertion is fashionable that we are living in a type of society that no longer obeys the laws of classical capitalism (namely the primacy of industrial production and the omnipresence of class struggle) and that therefore Marxism is outmoded. In contrast with this postmodernist/post-structuralist view Mandel argues that the contemporary form of capitalism represents the purest form of capitalism to have emerged.

There has been a prodigious expansion of capitalism into hitherto uncommodified areas: for example the penetration and colonization of Nature and the Unconscious, that is to say, the destruction of the pre-capitalist agriculture and the rise of the media and the advertising industry.

Jameson's main political concepts, inherited from Lukács and the Frankfurt School, are those of reification and commodification. He contends that aesthetic production has become integrated into commodity production:

> This whole global, yet American, postmodern culture is the internal and superstructural expression of a whole new wave of American military and economic domination throughout the world: in this sense, as throughout class history, the underside of culture is blood, death and horror.[6]

Jameson is deeply concerned about the incapacity of our minds (at least at present) to map the great global multinational and decentred communicational network in which we find ourselves caught as individual subjects. He describes how we all, in one way or another, dimly feel that not only local forms of cultural resistance but also even overtly political interventions are somehow secretly disarmed and reabsorbed by a system of which they themselves might well be considered a part, since they can achieve no distance from it.

While the high modernists were very interested in time and memory it seems that now our daily life, our cultural languages, are dominated by the category of space rather than time. Jameson uses the metaphor of an alienated city to refer to a space in which people are unable to map in their mind either their own positions or the urban totality in which they find themselves. He argues that we should map our individual social relationship to local, national and international class realities, a process that requires us to co-ordinate existential data, the empirical position of the subject, with theoretical conceptions of the totality. We need to develop an aesthetic of cognitive mapping, a pedagogical political culture which seeks to endow the individual subject with some new heightened sense of its place in the global system.

While reading this you may have been asking, 'What has all this to do with me?' I agree with Antonio Gramsci's remark that 'everything is political, even philosophy and philosophies'. Texts, philosophies and so forth acquire power through what Gramsci describes as diffusion, dissemination into and hegemony over the world of 'common sense': 'In the realm of culture and of thought each production exists not only to earn a place for itself but to displace, win out over, others.'[7] I suggest that the controversy about modernism and postmodernism should be seen in the context of ideological struggle. This debate is, implicitly, about the status, the validity of Marxism. The project of modernity is one with that of the Enlightenment. And Marxism is a child of the Enlightenment. But the postmodernists declare that progress is myth. Obviously each position on or within postmodernism is marked by our political interests and values.[8] How we conceive of postmodernism is central to how we re-present the past, the present, and the future to ourselves and others.

A characteristic of human beings is that they make a distinction between 'the real' and 'the ideal'. By the real I mean an awareness of the present situation, and by the ideal, some notion of what life, the world, could be like. Human beings have a sense of what is possible in the future and they have the hope that tomorrow will be better than today. Marxists not only have this hope, this orientation towards the future, but they try to understand the world, to develop a critical consciousness of it, and try to develop strategies for changing it. Of course, they realize that progress is uneven, not unilinear; because of the nature of contradiction there are inevitably negative aspects, sad reversals and painful losses. Marxists struggle for a better future for all, but they know that this does not mean that progress is guaranteed or that the processes of the dialectic will lead to the Perfect. I believe that it is important for people to support the Enlightenment project because education is closely connected with the notion of a change of consciousness; gaining a wider, deeper understanding of the world represents a change for the better. And this, in turn, implies some belief in a worthwhile future. Without

this presupposition the education of people would be
pointless.

RE-VISION

Before I conclude I would like to give a brief 'précis' of the
ground covered in the foregoing chapters. Its main purpose
is not to tell you 'to read the chapters in a certain way' but
to encourage you to reflect—and comment—on the issues
raised. I began by discussing the three most influential post-
structuralists: Lacan, Derrida and Foucault. Chapter 1, a
general introduction to Lacan and his theory of psychoanalysis, suggested that Lacanian theory offered a way of thinking
about the social and the linguistic construction of the self.
We urgently need a model that overcomes the opposition
between the individual and the social, because no political
revolution can be completed until the 'character structures'
inherited from prerevolutionary society are transformed. I
think that a (revised) Lacanian model of the subject could
perhaps help us to conceive of a different signification, a
different subjectivity, and a different symbolic order.

There was an account of Derrida's thought in Chapter 2.
I outlined his arguments against Lacan and other thinkers
and then described his views on Freud, who influenced
Derrida's thinking on reading texts, and Nietzsche, who
influenced his understanding of the nature and function of
metaphor. I argued that metaphors determine to a large
extent what we can think in any field and that they shape
what we do. Finally, after situating metaphor in the
context of political and ideological struggle, I discussed the
relationship between deconstruction and Marxism.

Chapter 3 focused on Foucault, a writer whose works are
based on a vision of history derived from Nietzsche. I gave
an exposition of Foucault's work which is largely concerned
with the growth of the modern sciences and the process of
modernization. The relationship between knowledge and
power, another Nietzschean theme, was also discussed. For
Foucault knowledge is not neutral or objective but is a

product of power relations. Power in modern times is productive, it operates through the construction of new capacities and modes of activity. After describing some of the similarities and differences between Foucault and Althusser, I presented Foucault's arguments against Marxism. I stressed the point that Foucault and his many followers, both in France and in this country, have been vigorously propagating the view that Marxism is authoritarian and outmoded. Nietzsche's thought has influenced Foucault so deeply that it is not surprising that he rejects Marx's view of economics, history, politics and method. For Foucault it is no longer feasible to conceptualize relations of power in terms of the state, class struggle, relations of production and capitalist exploitation.

In Chapter 4 I outlined some of the important differences between the philosophies of Nietzsche and Hegel and stressed the fact that Nietzsche's thought—his antipathy to any system, his rejection of the Hegelian view of history as progress, his preoccupation with the subjective—is central to the post-structuralist's anti-Marxist stance. I introduced some of the ideas of writers like Deleuze and Guattari (who see in Marxism an instrument of domination and who glorify spontaneity, subjectivity and intensity), Foucault, Lyotard and others who always emphasize the local, the heterogeneous and the fragmentary. I then discussed the 'new philosophers' who also draw heavily on Nietzsche's thought and combine certain elements and themes from the work of post-structuralist writers.

I began Chapter 5 with an exposition of Lyotard's thesis: as knowledge is now becoming the principal force of production, we should seriously consider the changing nature of knowledge as computerized societies enter what is known as the postmodern age. It was explained that the debate about modernism and postmodernism is (partly) about the arts, and so there was a discussion about the role of art in bourgeois society. Postmodernists/post-structuralists believe that the modern narratives of the emancipation of the working class, the classless society, have lost credibility. Marxism is outmoded.

Post-structuralists, I maintained, are antagonistic to the

concept of totality and in its stead emphasize fragmentation. Everything consists of fragments; and as they do not recognize a unity against which the fragments can be measured they tend towards relativism. The post-structuralists also emphasize the local and the contingent and have a hatred of all overarching theories. With some thinkers, such as Derrida and Foucault, this had led to a conceptual relativism so strong as to seem self-defeating. It is not surprising, then, that Lyotard believes that power is increasingly becoming the criterion of truth.

Derrida, Foucault and other post-structuralists challenge the idea that knowledge 'grows' or 'progresses' in any more than a purely quantitative sense. (One paradox of their work is that although they repudiate any notion of a general theory, their theory does express a general view about the nature of knowledge.) Not only do they give up humanism's belief in epistemological progress, they also give up its belief in social historical progress. Derrida, Foucault and other modern Nietzscheans see history as 'ending' in the sense of dying. Having lost faith in the progessive character of history, they are reacting against the thinkers of the Enlightenment. They assert that the Enlightenment project of modernity has failed. In opposition to this view it was argued that Marxism, a child of the eighteenth-century Enlightenment, is committed to education, rationality and progress.

Of course, I agree with Jameson's point that we need to recover a history of society which hitherto has been misrepresented or rendered invisible. We need to develop a pedagogical political culture which seeks to endow the individual subject with some new heightened sense of its place in local, national, and international realities. This is an extremely difficult project. In contemporary societies there is a struggle for interpretative power, and the prevailing ideologies limit the means by which individuals understand their material experiences. The modern culture-industry robs individuals of 'languages' for interpreting self and world by denying them the media for organizing their own experiences. We urgently need to provide individuals and social groups with public 'spaces', in which they can deal with subliminally felt experiences and learn to understand these experiences on a more conscious, critical level.[9] History, literature, storytelling, therefore, have important functions because they provide discourses and opportunities for dealing with experiences by discussing them. Only experiences confirmed and corroborated through discussion and coped with as collective experience can be said to be truly experienced. According to this view consciousness is the historically concrete production of meaning, and every historical situation contains ideological ruptures and offers possibilites for social transformation.

Notes

INTRODUCTION

1 For a good introduction to these debates see K. Soper, *Humanism and Anti-Humanism*, London, Hutchinson, 1986.
2 C. Lévi-Strauss, *The Savage Mind*, London, Weidenfeld & Nicolson, 1966. The attack, ch. 9 of the above book, is published as 'History and Dialectic' in R. and F. DeGeorge (eds), *The Structuralists from Marx to Lévi-Strauss*, New York, Anchor Books, 1972.
3 F. de Saussure, *Course in General Linguistics*, London, Fontana/Collins, 1974.
4 J. Lacan, *Écrits: A Selection*, London, Tavistock, 1977, p. 154.
5 See J. Culler, *Structuralist Poetics*, London, Routledge & Kegan Paul, 1975, p. 247.
6 It is important to differentiate clearly structuralism, structuralist Marxism and post-structuralism. By putting these three together as theories of structure (as opposed to action) many writers fail to underline the profoundly anti-Marxist nature of post-structuralism. See, for example, I. Craib, *Modern Social Theory: From Parsons to Habermas*, Brighton, Harvester Press, 1984.

CHAPTER 1   LACAN AND PSYCHOANALYSIS

1 S. Turkle, *Psychoanalytic Politics, Jacques Lacan and Freud's French Revolution*, London, Burnett Books, 1979, p. 67.
2 The article 'Freud and Lacan' is in L. Althusser, *Lenin and Philosophy and Other Essays*, London, New Left Books, 1971.
3 J. Lacan, *De la psychose paranoiaque dans ses rapports avec la personnalité*, Paris, Éditions du Seuil, 1975.
4 See J. Mitchell, *Psychoanalysis and Feminism*, London, Penguin Books, 1974.

5 S. Freud, *Beyond the Pleasure Principle*, Standard Edition, vol. 18, London, Hogarth Press, 1955.

6 J. Lacan, *Écrits: A Selection*, London, Tavistock, 1977, pp. 1–7.

7 A. Lemaire, *Jacques Lacan*, London, Routledge & Kegan Paul, 1977, p. 92.

8 Ibid., pp. 156–60.

9 Ibid., p. 166.

10 When the psychoanalytic session begins the analysand talks of himself or herself as an object. This is what Lacan calls 'empty speech'. In contrast, 'full speech' is when the subject coincides with the object, when *who* is talking coincides with *what* is being talked about.

11 See Laplanche and Leclair, 'The Unconscious: a Psychoanalytic Study', *Yale French Studies*, no. 48, pp. 118–75; also A. Lemaire, op. cit., ch. 9.

12 Lacan, *Écrits*, p. 12.

13 J. Gallop, *Feminism and Psychoanalysis: The Daughter's Seduction*, London, Macmillan, 1982, p. 12.

14 Lacan, *Écrits*, p. 134.

15 D.W. Winnicott, *Playing and Reality*, London, Penguin, 1974, pp. 130–8.

16 Lacan, *Écrits*, p. 2.

17 J.-P. Sartre, *Being and Nothingness*, London, Methuen, 1957.

18 Lacan, *Écrits*, p. 119.

19 D. Archard, *Consciousness and the Unconscious*, London, Hutchinson, 1984, p. 25. This useful book contains a brief outline of Freud's theory and Sartre's critique of it, a clear exposition of Lacan and, finally, Timpanaro's critique of the 'Freudian slip'.

20 Lacan, *Écrits*, p. 161.

21 Ibid., p. 281.

22 A. Kojève, *Introduction to the Reading of Hegel: Lectures on the Phenomenology of Spirit*, assembled by Raymond Queneau, New York, Basic Books, Inc., 1969. It should be noted that for Hegel human consciousness was an aspect of *Geist*. Kojève brings Hegel down to earth and stresses the elements of labour, language and struggle.

23 Ibid., p. 37.

24 Ibid., p. 228.

25 Ibid., p. 206.

26 Ibid., p. 220.

27 Ibid., p. 58.

28 Lacan makes a distinction between need (a purely organic energy) and desire, the active principle of the physical processes. Desire always lies both beyond and before demand. To say that desire is beyond demand means that it transcends it, that it is eternal because it is impossible to satisfy. It is forever insatiable since it refers back to the ineffable, to the unconscious desire and the absolute lack it conceals. Every human action, even the most altruistic, derives from a desire for recognition by the Other, from a wish for self-recognition in some

form or another. Desire is the desire for desire, the desire of the Other.

29 J. Lacan, *The Four Fundamental Concepts of Psycho-analysis*, London, Penguin, 1979, pp. 196–7, 205. A useful account of the myth is given by K. Silverman, *The Subject of Semiotics*, Oxford University Press, 1983, p. 151.

30 For a discussion of Lacan's phallocentrism and its implications see J. Mitchell and J. Rose, *Feminine Sexuality*, London, Macmillan, 1982.

31 Jameson believes that both psychoanalysis and Marxism depend fundamentally on history and story-telling. See F. Jameson, 'Imaginary and Symbolic in Lacan: Marxism, Psychoanalytic Criticism, and the Problem of the Subject', *Yale French Studies*, 1977, nos. 55–6, pp. 338–95.

32 Wilhelm Reich (1897–1957), a prophet of sexual revolution, asserted that mental health is dependent on the capacity to experience orgasm and that mental illness is the result of inhibition of the capacity to experience orgasm. See C. Rycroft, *Reich*, London, Fontana, 1971.

33 See 'Introduction to Irigaray', *Ideology and Consciousness*, May 1977, no. 1, pp. 57–76. A good introduction to French feminist theory is T. Moi's *Sexual/Textual Politics*, London, Methuen, 1985.

34 The family is usually regarded as the central mediatory institution between the individual and the social realm. See, for example, M. Poster, *Critical Theory of the Family*, London, Pluto Press, 1978, ch. 2. See also ch. 4 for an account of Lacan.

35 For an extended discussion of this point see B. Ollman, *Alienation*, Cambridge University Press, 1976 (2nd edition), pp. 245–50.

CHAPTER 2   DERRIDA AND DECONSTRUCTION

1 J. Derrida, *Of Grammatology*, Baltimore and London, Johns Hopkins University Press, 1976; *Speech and Phenomena, and Other Essays on Husserl's Theory of Signs*, Evanston, Northwestern University Press, 1973; *Writing and Difference*, London, Routledge & Kegan Paul, 1978.

2 See T. Eagleton, *Literary Theory: An Introduction*, Oxford, Basil Blackwell, 1983, pp. 127–34.

3 Derrida's arguments are largely based on the chapter 'A Writing Lesson' in Lévi-Strauss's *Tristes Tropiques*, London, Penguin, 1976, p. 385.

4 For critiques of Saussure, Rousseau, Lévi-Strauss see Derrida, *Of Grammatology*.

5 Derrida finds the same powerful metaphors at work in Husserl's meditations on language and thought; see Derrida's *Speech and Phenomena*.

6 See Derrida's 'Freud and the Scene of Writing' in *Writing and*

Difference, p. 196. Derrida traces the emergence of the metaphor of writing through three texts placed on a thirty-year span in Freud's career: 'Project for a Scientific Psychology' (1985), *The Interpretation of Dreams* (1899), and *Note on the Mystic Writing Pad* (1925).

7 J. Habermas, *Knowledge and Human Interests*, London, Heinemann Educational Books, 1972, chapters 10–12.

8 Readers should be reminded that proper names such as Nietzsche, Freud, Heidegger are a convenient fiction. For Derrida the names of authors indicate neither identities nor causes. Proper names are serviceable 'metonymic contractions' that refer to problems.

9 Nietzsche faces reflexive concerns that have parallels with modern relativism, but instead of stepping back, which he regards as impossible, he endorses paradox and incorporates reflexivity into his own writing. See H. Lawson, *Reflexivity: The Post-modern Predicament*, London, Hutchinson, 1985, p. 32.

10 Nietzsche, 'On Truth and Falsity in their Ultramoral Sense', in O. Levy (ed.), *The Complete Works of Friedrich Nietzsche*, New York, 1964.

11 G. Lakoff and M. Johnson, *Metaphors We Live By*, Chicago, University of Chicago Press, 1980.

12 C. Hill, *Reformation to Industrial Revolution*, London, Penguin, 1967; quoted by Lawton in Taylor, op. cit.

13 M. Foucault, *Power/Knowledge, Selected Interviews and Other Writings 1972–1977*, edited by C. Gordon, Brighton, Harvester Press, 1980, pp. 68–70.

14 Gayatri Chakravorty Spivak, 'Translator's Preface', Derrida, *Of Grammatology*, p. lxxv. I have found this preface lucid and most helpful.

15 Ibid., p. lxxvii.

16 But, as Rée has pointed out, Derrida is so preoccupied with metaphor that he fails to remember such literary processes as narrative, story and plot. See J. Rée, 'Metaphor and Metaphysics: The End of Philosophy and Derrida', *Radical Philosophy*, 38, Summer 1984, p. 33. For an introduction to Derrida see D.C. Woods in *Radical Philosophy*, 21, Spring 1979.

17 Eagleton, op. cit., p. 138.

18 Ibid., p. 147.

19 V. Leitch, *Deconstructive Criticism, An advanced introduction*, London, Hutchinson, 1983, p. 246.

20 Post-structuralists, generally, favour authors who shift the textuality of their production, the ambiguity and the plurality of meanings, to the foreground. They admire authors like Rimbaud, Lautréamont, Robbe-Grillet, Joyce.

21 E.W. Said, 'Opponents, Audiences, Constituencies and Community', in H. Foster (ed.), *Postmodern Culture*, London, Pluto Press, 1985, p. 143.

22 Eagleton, op. cit., p. 148.

23 Lawson, op. cit., p. 113–15.

24 F. Jameson, *Marxism and Form*, Princeton University Press, 1971. See the note on p. 409. See also M. Ryan, *Marxism and Deconstruction*, Baltimore, Johns Hopkins University Press, 1982.

25 C. Norris, *Deconstruction: Theory and Practice*, London, Methuen, 1982, p. 84.

26 T. Eagleton, *Walter Benjamin or Towards a Revolutionary Criticism*, London, New Left Books, 1981, p. 137. Eagleton may have since changed his mind. In *Literary Theory*, 1983, he writes: 'The widespread opinion that deconstruction denies the existence of anything but discourse, or affirms a realm of pure difference in which all meaning and identity dissolves, is a travesty of Derrida's own work and of *the most productive work which has followed from it*' (p. 148, my italics).

CHAPTER 3   FOUCAULT AND THE SOCIAL SCIENCES

1 M. Foucault, 'Nietzsche, Genealogy, History', in D.F. Bouchard (ed.), *Language, Counter-Memory, Practice: Selected Essays and Interviews*, Oxford, Blackwell, 1977.

2 M. Foucault, *Madness and Civilization*, London, Tavistock, 1967.

3 Ibid., p. 46.

4 Ibid., p. 48.

5 Ibid., p. 64.

6 Ibid., p. 247.

7 Ibid., p. 254.

8 Derrida has criticized Foucault for still being confined within the structuralist science of investigation through oppositions. See the essay entitled 'Cogito and the History of Madness' in J. Derrida, *Writing and Difference*, London, Routledge & Kegan Paul, 1978, p. 34.

9 M. Foucault, *The Birth of the Clinic*, London, Tavistock, 1973.

10 M. Foucault, *The Order of Things*, London, Tavistock, 1970; *The Archaeology of Knowledge*, London, Tavistock, 1972.

11 M. Foucault, *Power/Knowledge, Selected Interviews and Other Writings 1972–1977*, edited by C. Gordon, Brighton, Harvester Press, 1980, p. 115.

12 M. Foucault (ed.), *I, Pierre Rivière ... A Case of Parricide in the 19th Century*, London, Penguin, 1978.

13 M. Foucault, *Discipline and Punish*, London, Penguin, 1977.

14 Foucault, *Power/Knowledge*, p. 47.

15 Instrumental reason separates fact and value; it is concerned with discovering *how* to do things, not with what should be done. And so public affairs come to be regarded not as areas of discussion and choice but as technical problems to be solved by experts employing an instrumental rationality. The concept is explored in T. Adorno and M. Horkheimer, *Dialectic of the Enlightenment*, New York,

Herder and Herder, 1972, and M. Horkheimer, *Eclipse of Reason*, New York, Seabury Press, 1974. The latter is a popularization of the former book.

16 M. Foucault, *The History of Sexuality; Volume One: An Introduction*, London, Allen Lane, 1979. The second volume is called *L'usage des plaisirs*, *The Use of Pleasure*, London, Allen Lane, 1986; the third volume is *Le souci de soi*, *The Concern for Self*. Foucault died in June 1984, aged 57.

17 Foucault, *Power/Knowledge*, p. 98.

18 F. Nietzsche, *On the Genealogy of Morals*, New York, Vintage Books, 1969.

19 P. Dews, 'Power and Subjectivity in Foucault', *New Left Review*, No. 144, March–April 1984, p. 72.

20 L. Althusser, 'Ideology and Ideological State Apparatuses', in *Lenin and Philosophy and Other Essays*, London, New Left Books, 1971, p. 167.

21 For an excellent introduction to this debate see K. Soper, *Humanism and Anti-Humanism*, London, Hutchinson, 1986.

22 L. Althusser, *For Marx*, London, Penguin, 1969; *Reading Capital*, London, New Left Books, 1970. The latter contains a useful glossary of Althusserian terms.

23 M. Cousins and A. Hussain, *Michel Foucault*, London, Macmillan, 1984.

24 T. Benton, *The Rise and Fall of Structural Marxism: Louis Althusser and his Influence*, London, Macmillan, 1984. Benton suggests that the cognitive claims of science and its culturally produced character can perhaps be reconciled by a realist view of science, currently being developed by Roy Bhaskar and others, a view which was unavailable to Althusser. See R. Bhaskar, *A Realist Theory of Science*, Brighton, Harvester Press, 1978; *The Possibility of Naturalism*, Brighton, Harverster Press, 1979.

25 Foucault, *The Order of Things*, pp. 261–2. And see *Power/Knowledge*, p. 76.

26 Foucault, *Power/Knowledge*, p. 142.

27 Ibid., p. 62.

28 Ibid., p. 65.

29 Ibid., p. 85.

30 See M. Philp, 'Michel Foucault', in Q. Skinner (ed.), *The Return of Grand Theory in the Human Sciences*, Cambridge University Press, 1985, p. 79.

31 For the view that Foucault does not interrogate, as Marx did, the conditions of his own thought see M. Poster, *Foucault, Marxism and History*, Cambridge, Polity Press, 1984, p. 155.

32 Foucault, *Power/Knowledge*, p. 62.

33 Ibid., p. 203.

34 Ibid., pp. 207–8.

35 Ibid., p. 138.

36 See B. Jessop, *Nicos Poulantzas: State, Class and Strategy*, London, Macmillan, 1985.

37 See M. Ignatieff, 'State, Civil Society and Total Institutions: A Critique of Recent Social Histories of Punishment', in S. Cohen and A. Scull (eds), *Social Control and the State*, Oxford, Basil Blackwell, 1983.
38 N. Poulantzas, *State, Power, Socialism*, London, New Left Books, 1978. It has been said that this book is possibly the best exploration to date of the implications of Foucault's work for Marxist theory and politics; see B. Smart, *Foucault, Marxism and Critique*, London, Routledge & Kegan Paul, 1984, pp. 96–107.
39 Foucault, *Power/Knowledge*, p. 193.
40 Ibid., pp. 143–4.

CHAPTER 4 SOME CURRENTS WITHIN POST-STRUCTURALISM

1 G. Deleuze and F. Guattari, *Anti-Oedipus: Capitalism and Schizophrenia*, New York, Viking Press, 1977. See also G. Deleuze, *Nietzsche and Philosophy*, London, Athlone Press, 1983.
2 Deleuze and Guattari, op. cit., p. 131.
3 J.-J. Lecercle, *Philosophy through the Looking-Glass: Language, Nonsense, Desire*, London, Hutchinson, 1985, p. 199.
4 V. Descombes, *Modern French Philosophy*, Cambridge University Press, p. 173.
5 We should note that both these modes of thought cut across the political divisions of left and right. See the remarkable book by M. Berman, *All That Is Solid Melts Into Air: The Experience of Modernity*, London, Verso, 1983, which is a brilliant study of modernization and modernism.
6 J. Habermas, 'The Entwinement of Myth and Enlightenment: Rereading *Dialectic of Enlightenment*', *New German Critique*, 26, 1982, p. 28.
7 M. Foucault, *The History of Sexuality*, London, Penguin, pp. 92–102.
8 See D. Howard, *The Marxian Legacy*, London, Macmillan, 1977. Chapter 9 is on Lefort and chapter 10 is on Castoriadis.
9 J.-F. Lyotard, *Discours/figure*, Paris, Klincksieck, 1971.
10 G. Lukács, *History of Class Consciousness*, London, Merlin Press, 1971.
11 L. Althusser, *For Marx*, London, Penguin, 1969, pp. 230, 248.
12 See E. Laclau, The Specificity of the Political, in *Politics and Ideology in Marxist Theory*, London, Verso, p. 51.
13 E.P. Thompson, *The Poverty of Theory and other essays*, London, Merlin Press, 1978. For a critical assessment of Thompson's work see P. Anderson, *Arguments within English Marxism*, London, Verso, 1980.
14 C. Claudin-Urondo, *Lenin and the Cultural Revolution*, Brighton, Harvester Press, 1977, p. 76.

15 For an elaboration of the points in this section see Barry Smart, *Foucault, Marxism and Critique*, London, Routledge & Kegan Paul, 1983.

16 B.-H. Lévy, *La barbarie à visage humain*, Paris, Grasset, 1977.

17 These Borromean knots are made of interlocking circles; when one is cut, the whole chain of circles becomes undone. They are described and illustrated in S. Turkle, *Psychoanalytic Politics: Jacques Lacan and Freud's French Revolution*, London, Burnett Books, 1979, p. 235.

18 This section is indebted to Peter Dews, 'The *Nouvelle Philosophie* and Foucault', *Economy and Society*, vol. 8, No. 2, May 1979. See also P. Dews, 'The "New Philosophers" and the End of Leftism', *Radical Philosophy*, No. 24, Spring 1980.

19 A. Glucksmann, *Les Maîtres penseurs*, Paris, Grasset, 1977.

20 These are the views of Jean-Marie Benoist, the author of *Marx est mort; The Structural Revolution*, London, Weidenfeld & Nicolson, 1978, and other works.

21 Even among British Marxists there is an increasing interest in religion. For example, Gareth Stedman-Jones has recently argued that socialism was religious before it was secular. In a sense, socialism was a post-Christian religion. See the work of Fourier and Saint-Simon.

22 T. Eagleton, *Literary Theory*, Oxford, Basil Blackwell, 1983, p. 142.

CHAPTER 5   POSTMODERNISM

1 J.-F. Lyotard, *The Postmodern Condition: A Report on Knowledge*, Manchester, Manchester University Press, 1984.

2 The term 'white-collar' is perhaps no longer useful as it puts together the well-paid positions at the top of the hierarchy and the mass of proletarianized workers. See the interesting chapter on clerical workers in H. Braverman, *Labour and Monopoly Capital*, New York, Monthly Review Press, 1974.

3 The important questions are: What is transmitted? Who does the transmission and to whom? Through what medium and in what form? With what effect? Only a coherent set of answers to these questions can form a viable educational policy.

4 L. Wittgenstein, *Philosophical Investigations*, Oxford, Basil Blackwell, 1958. I have found the following books helpful: A. Janik and S. Toulmin, *Wittgenstein's Vienna*, New York, Simon and Schuster, 1973; H. Pitkin, *Wittgenstein and Justice*, Los Angeles, University of California Press, 1972.

5 Those utterances which do not describe but 'do' something, e.g. 'naming', 'betting', 'marrying', etc., J.L. Austin calls *performatives*. For a short and clear introduction to these concepts see D. Silverman and B. Torode, *The Material Word: Some theories of language and its limits*, London, Routledge & Kegan Paul, 1980, chapters 3 and 9.

6 Lyotard, op. cit., p. 17.
7 Introductions to the philosophy of science include A.F. Chalmers, *What is this thing called Science?*, Milton Keynes, The Open University Press, 1978; R. Harré, *The Philosophies of Science*, Oxford University Press, 1972.
8 Fredric Jameson has cogently observed that Lyotard is rather unwilling to posit the disappearance of the great master narratives – they could have passed underground, as it were, and may still be influencing our thinking and acting unconsciously. This persistence of buried master narratives is what Jameson calls 'the political unconscious'.
9 Lyotard, op. cit., p. 37.
10 Ibid., p. 45. About this statement Eagleton contentiously remarks: 'It is not difficult, then, to see a relation between the philosophy of J.L. Austin and IBM, or between the various neo-Nietzscheanisms of a post-structuralist epoch and Standard Oil.' See T. Eagleton, Capitalism, Modernism and Postmodernism', *New Left Review*, No. 152, July/August 1985, p. 63.
11 But resistance to change has a use. See T. Kuhn, *The Structure of Scientific Revolutions*, Chicago, University of Chicago Press, 1970, p. 65. For a discussion of Kuhn's views see I. Lakatos and A. Musgrave (eds), *Criticism and the Growth of Knowledge*, Cambridge University Press, 1970.
12 P. Bürger, *Theory of the Avant-Garde*, Manchester University Press, 1984. I would like to suggest that the 'Foreword' to this book be read after the text.
13 H. Marcuse, 'On the affirmative character of culture', in *Negations, Essays in Critical Theory*, London, Penguin Books, 1986.
14 There may be several avant-gardes. Bürger's term 'the historic avant-garde' refers to the historical uniqueness of the avant-garde movements of the 1920s such as Dadaism and Surrealism.
15 P. Bürger, op. cit., p. 66.
16 Bürger feels that the avant-gardistes' attempt to reintegrate art into the life process is itself a contradictory endeavour. An art no longer distinct from the praxis of life but wholly absorbed in it will lose the capacity to criticize it, along with its distance. Perhaps the distance between art and praxis of life is a necessary free space within which alternatives to what exists can become conceivable? See Bürger, op. cit., p. 54.
17 See J. Habermas, 'Modernity Versus Postmodernity', *New German Critique*, 22, Winter 1981.
18 D. Bell, *The Cultural Contradictions of Capitalism*, New York, Basic Books, 1976.
19 Lyotard, op. cit., p. xxiii.
20 Lyotard in an interview with Christian Descamps.
21 Lyotard, op. cit., p. 37.
22 See the work of the anthropologist Robin Horton, for example, 'African Traditional Thought and Western Science', in B. Wilson (ed.), *Rationality*, Oxford, Basil Blackwell, 1970.

23 F. Jameson, 'Postmodernism, or the Cultural Logic of Capital', *New Left Review*, No. 146, July/August 1984.

24 Bürger, op. cit., p. 69.

25 For debates between Ernst Bloch, Georg Lukács, Bertolt Brecht, Walter Benjamin and Theodor Adorno see *Aesthetics and Politics*, with an afterword by Fredric Jameson, London, New Left Books, 1977.

26 For a concise description of Adorno's position see G. Rose, *The Melancholy Science: An Introduction to the Thought of Theodor W. Adorno*, London, Macmillan, 1978. See particularly chapter 6, 'The Dispute over Modernism'.

27 See W. Benjamin, 'What is Epic Theatre?', in *Illuminations*, London, Fontana, 1973.

28 The rhetoric of liberation has been denounced with passionate ambivalence by M. Foucault in *History of Sexuality; Volume One: An Introduction*, London, Allen Lane, 1979. Totality and totalization have also been rejected by many contemporary theorists; see M. Jay, *Marxism and Totality: The Adventures of a Concept from Lukács to Habermas*, Oxford, Polity Press, 1984.

29 Lyotard, op. cit., p. 60.

30 R. Rorty, 'Habermas and Lyotard on Post-modernity', *Praxis International*, vol. 4, No. 1, April 1984, p. 40.

CONCLUSION

1 F. Jameson, *The Political Unconscious: Narrative as a Socially Symbolic Act*, London, Methuen, 1981. For a useful introduction to this book see W. Dowling, *Jameson, Althusser, Marx*, London, Methuen, 1984.

2 Jameson claims that political criticism is the absolute horizon of all interpretation. Literary works are to be grasped not primarily as objective structures but as *symbolic* practices.

3 It has been remarked that Jameson's typical intellectual habit is to consider two or more apparently incompatible theses, show how each is symptomatic of a real historical condition and thus try to dissolve the contradictions between them. See T. Eagleton, 'The Idealism of American Criticism', *New Left Review*, No. 127, May/June 1981, pp. 60–5.

4 Jameson, *New Left Review*, No. 146, p. 58.

5 E. Mandel, *Late Capitalism*, London, Verso, 1978, p. 184.

6 Jameson, *New Left Review*, No. 146, p. 57.

7 For a study of the genealogy of the concept of hegemony see E. Laclau and C. Mouffe, *Hegemony and Socialist Strategy: Towards a Radical Democratic Politics*, London, Verso, 1985.

8 See the articles by Habermas, Jameson and Said and others in the anthology edited by H. Foster, *Postmodern Culture*, London, Pluto Press, 1985.

9 O. Negt and A. Kluge, *Öffentlichkeit und Erfahrung*, Frankfurt-on-Main, 1972.

Notes on Further Reading

This book is intended as a starting point for further thought. If you want to explore a topic look up the references in the *Notes*, where I have mentioned all the texts I have used, quoted or discussed. There are, however, some additional books that I would like to mention.

LACAN AND PSYCHOANALYSIS

For a most useful exposition of Lacan's main writings see Bice Benvenuto and Roger Kennedy, *The Works of Jacques Lacan: An Introduction*, London, Free Association Books, 1986. The book discusses Lacan's texts from the early works to the works of the mid-1970s in chronological order. Also helpful is Juliet Flower MacCannell, *Figuring Lacan: Criticism and the Cultural Unconscious*, London, Croom Helm, 1986. An indispensable (but expensive) book is Jean Laplanche and Jean Baptiste Pontalis, *The Language of Psychoanalysis*, London, The Hogarth Press, 1973; this is a work of encyclopaedic scholarship, a dictionary of articles which discusses almost 300 Freudian concepts. The key theme of Elizabeth Wright, *Psychoanalytic Criticism: Theory in Practice*, London, Methuen, 1984, is the relationship between different psychoanalytic theories and theories of art and literature. It is an excellent introduction to Freud, Klein and Lacan.

Is it true that Lacan spent so much of his time on theory

that he lost touch with clinical practice? And is the theory so intellectual that it neglects emotion and affect? I found Stuart Schneiderman, *Jacques Lacan: the Death of an Intellectual Hero*, Harvard University Press, 1983, a valuable account on this and other matters. He writes sensitively about death and its symbolization, the relation of the dead and the living, and the importance of Sophocles' *Antigone* for our understanding of ethical conduct. The author describes the organization of the École Freudienne and justifies Lacan's practice of the short session.

While Lacan does not neglect the question of power I think it could be said that he does not seriously consider that there may be systems of meanings that promote or mask relations of force. Freud held the Enlightenment view that the conquest of the irrational by the rational, of compulsion by freedom was possible. Lacan, on the other hand, seems to think that any sort of autonomy or self-determination is not possible. Is he justified in thinking this?

DERRIDA AND DECONSTRUCTION

Throughout his work Derrida hints at a complicity between the fundamental assumptions of Western thought and the violences and repressions which have characterized Western history, but the nature of this link is never really made explicit. One major reason for this is the disanalogy between texts and institutions, and Derrida's consequent inability to give an appropriate account of the latter. On the one hand, Derrida recognizes that institutions are powerful forces but this view contradicts his contention that there is no 'outside of the text'. Surely deconstruction is concerned with logical contradictions, to which political antagonisms cannot be reduced?

For an opposing view see the lucid study by Christopher Norris, *Derrida*, London, Fontana, 1987. According to Norris, Derrida is against the idea that there is some realm of pure textuality beyond the claims of political or ethical life. Derrida demands that we try to think beyond such disabling assumptions as those which would treat 'the world' and 'the text' in binary, disjunctive terms. He tries to demonstrate that Derrida's readings of Nietzsche and Freud insist on the 'worldly' consequences that follow from the act of writing, and he goes on to claim that there is an ethical dimension to Derrida's writing. In his view, deconstruction may have had such a great impact in the United States because it possesses a written constitution whose principles are yet open to all manner of far-reaching judicial review (for example, racial equality, civil rights, etc.). This gives a political edge to questions of textual and interpretative theory that they do not have in the British cultural context. Norris is particularly clear on the differences between Derrida and Foucault. Foucault's extreme epistemological scepticism leads him to equate knowledge with power, and hence to regard all forms of enlightened progress (in psychiatry, sexual attitudes or penal reform) as signs of increasing social control. Derrida, by contrast, insists that there is no opting out of that post-Kantian enlightenment tradition. It is only by working persistently *within* that tradition, but *against* some of its ruling ideas, that thought can muster the resistance required for an effective critique of existing institutions.

FOUCAULT AND THE SOCIAL SCIENCES

Foucault's work is attracting increasing attention, and there are a number of helpful commentaries. I recommend the selection of writings in Paul Rabinow, ed., *The Foucault Reader*, Harmondsworth, Penguin, 1986. The book by Hubert Dreyfus and Paul Rabinow, *Michel Foucault: Beyond Structuralism and Hermeneutics*, Brighton, Harvester Press, 1982, is a clear exposition. Part II which deals with the shift in Foucault's work from discourse to power is particularly useful. The authors continually compare Foucault's thought with that of Heidegger, Wittgenstein and Kuhn. There is, indeed, a striking similarity between Kuhn's account of normal science and Foucault's account of normalizing society. However, the authors tend to be uncritical and completely ignore the political implications of Foucault's work. A well-known book is Mark Cousins and Athar Hussein, *Michael Foucault*, London, Macmillan, 1984. Peter Dew's scholarly book, *Logics of Disintegration: Poststructuralist Thought and the Claims of Critical Theory*, London Verso, 1987, contains an excellent account of Foucault's views on power, subjectivity, and knowledge. There is no doubt that Foucault's intention is to dissolve the philosophical link—inherited by the Marxist tradition from German idealism—between consciousness, self-reflection and freedom. He wants to deny that there remains any progressive political potential in the ideal of the autonomous subject. Foucault gives a positive account of power but if the concept is to have a critical, political edge, there must be some principle, force or entity which 'power' crushes or subdues, and whose release from this repression is considered desirable. He neglects to tell us that which modern power represses. As Foucault cannot define what power operates against, his theory of power loses all explanatory content.

The validity of Foucault's ideas and the coherence of his position are also the main themes of the book edited by David Hoy, *Foucault: A Critical Reader*, Oxford, Basil Blackwell, 1986. It contains essays by Dreyfus and Rabinow, Hacking, Jay, Rorty, Said, Habermas and others. The most critical book is by J.G. Merquior. Merquior calls Foucault a neo-anarchist, and accuses him of negativism and irrationalism. (See J.G. Merquior, *Foucault*, London, Fontana, 1985.) He argues that in Foucault's work the historical evidence is too selective and distorted and that his interpretations are too sweeping and biased. He is devoid of any vision of non-alienated social relations. And, of course, Foucault tries to demonstrate the radical discontinuity in history. But, if one denies any kind of continuity in history, then how is one to explain the possibility of writing history?

POST-STRUCTURALISM AND POSTMODERNISM

Richard Harland, *Superstructuralism*, London, Methuen, 1987, is a clear exposition of structuralism and post-structuralism but, like many other books on these topics, it ignores the fact that ideas have a *political* dimension, that they arise in certain contexts and have certain social and ideological effects.

For post-structuralists, unity and universality are inherently oppressive and any move which promotes their disintegration is to be approved. It is assumed that once the aspiration to universality is abandoned, what will be left is a harmonious plurality of unmediated perspectives. But this sort of Nietzschean pluralism or perpectivism is fundamentally inconsistent because, in fact, the right to difference can only be upheld by universal principles.

There is a useful discussion of Nietzsche, the chief forerunner of 'postmodern' reactions against the spirit of modern culture, in J.G. Merquior, *From Prague to Paris: A Critique of Structuralist and Post-Structuralist Thought*, London, Verso, 1986.

The book by Jean-François Lyotard and Jean Loup Thébaud, *Just Gaming*, Manchester University Press, 1986, is interesting because it represents a break with Lyotard's earlier Nietzscheanism. In the book Lyotard states that it is not true that the search for intensities or things of that type can ground politics because there is the problem of injustice. (Indeed, the book should be entitled 'Just about Justice'.) There is an excellent discussion of Lyotard's *early* work in the book I mentioned above, Peter Dews's *Logics of Disintegration*. Despite the distinction between the vocabulary of forces and power and that of libido and drives, the homology between the arguments of Lyotard and Foucault is unmistakable. They both stress that life cannot be grasped from any single, comprehensive perspective. In both cases, it is Nietzsche who provides the inspiration for a post-Hegelian and post-Marxist position.

For a useful overview of this area—from Sartre, through structuralism, to post-structuralism—see Vincent Descombes, *Modern French Philosophy*, Cambridge University Press, 1980.

For post-modernists it is the project of the Enlightenment that has to be deconstructed, the autonomous epistemological and moral subject that has to be decentred; the nostalgia for unity, totality and foundations that has to be overcome; and the tyranny of representational thought and universal truth that has to be defeated. As a result of this frontal attack there has been a breakup of any consensus as to what philosophy is. See, for example, Kenneth Baynes, James Bohman and Thomas McCarthy (eds), *After Philosophy: End or Transformation*, The MIT Press, 1987, which contains essays by Derrida, Foucault, Lyotard and others.

For both Lyotard and Foucault the fundamental object of attack is Hegelian Marxism. They are both implicitly but insistently against the Enlightenment tradition. Habermas, in contrast, is critical of the post-structuralists and defends the Enlightenment project. This fascinating debate can be followed in Richard J. Bernstein (ed.), *Habermas and Modernity*, Cambridge, Polity Press, 1985. Habermas sees himself as a rational progressivist and describes Foucault, Deleuze and Lyotard as 'neo-conservative'. While the post-structuralists see universalism as a mask of dogmatism, Habermas sees it as a rational guarantee of truth. There are critical analyses of Foucault, Derrida and Lyotard in Jürgen Habermas, *The Philosophical Discourse of Modernity*, Cambridge, Polity Press, 1988. Habermas argues that Foucault and others have replaced the repression/emancipation model founded by Marx and Freud with an analysis of a plurality of discursive and power formations which cannot be differentiated according to their validity. Habermas points out that demystifying culture only makes sense if we preserve a standard of truth capable of telling theory from ideology, knowledge from mystification. In short, while most of the post-structuralists systematically disparage the Enlightenment (and its heir Marxism), Habermas, wanting to 'complete' the Enlightenment project, stresses the possibility of human liberation.

Index

Adorno, Theodor, 77, 136–8, 156, 161
allegory, 135
Althusser, Louis, 1, 2, 3, 6, 55, 78, 83–5, 107, 157, 158
art, 126–9, 135, 137
avant-garde, 128–9, 135, 136–7

Benjamin, Walter, 135
Bentham, Jeremy, 75
Benton, Ted, 85, 157
Berman, Marshall, 105, 158
binary oppositions, 41, 43, 50, 56, 57, 59, 164
Brecht, Bertolt, 136, 137
Bürger, Peter, 126–9, 160

capitalism, 77, 114, 145, 146
class, 82, 87, 89, 93, 99, 100, 104, 110, 111, 112, 113, 143, 144
confession, 78, 79
confinement, 66–7

deconstruction, 34, 37, 40, 56, 57, 58–9, 60, 61, 62, 163, 164
Deleuze, Gilles, and Guattari, Félix, 96, 99–104, 158
demand (Lacan), 24, 25, 153

Derrida, Jacques, 2, 3, 12, 34–62, 96, 104, 154, 163, 164
Descartes, René, 1
desire (Lacan), 20, 21, 24, 25, 28, 30, 100, 101, 102, 104, 153, 154
Dews, Peter, 83, 157, 159, 165
différance (Derrida), 48
discourse, 70, 73, 80, 87, 88, 105, 144
dreams, 11, 18, 46, 47

Eagleton, Terry, 59, 61, 62, 154, 156, 159
education, 23, 124–5, 147
ego, 8, 11, 15, 17, 47
Enlightenment, 130, 131, 147, 163, 164, 167

fascism, 100
forte-da game, 9, 27, 28
Foucault, Michel, 2, 4, 54–5, 60, 63–95, 96, 105, 106, 111, 112, 133, 139, 140, 156, 157, 158, 164, 165, 167
fragmentation, 103, 107, 108, 132, 134, 144, 150

Freud, Sigmund, 6, 8, 9, 17, 18, 19, 20, 45, 46, 47, 49, 75, 78, 101, 105, 142, 153, 154, 155, 162, 163, 167

genealogy, 63–4, 88
Gramsci, Antonio, 147

Habermas, Jürgen, 105, 138, 155, 158, 167
Hegel, Georg W. F., 4, 6, 7, 16, 20, 22, 56, 63, 96–9, 132, 136, 153
Heidegger, Martin, 35, 49, 164
Hill, Christopher, 54
history, 2, 32, 63, 64, 81, 90, 93, 98–9, 106, 115, 141–3, 145, 150, 165
Husserl, Edmund, 4, 37, 38, 39, 49, 154

ideology, 40, 41, 83, 84, 85, 87, 88, 143, 144, 150
imaginary (Lacan), 27, 29, 30, 102, 112
intellectuals, 88, 105, 106, 109, 136
interpretation, 60, 101, 142, 143
intertextuality, 58, 59
Irigaray, Luce, 32

Jameson, Fredric, 32, 133, 141–6, 154, 156, 160, 161

Kant, Immanuel, 114
Klein, Melanie, 30, 162
knowledge, 70, 71, 73, 76, 81, 82, 85, 94, 97, 117, 118–25, 138, 149–50
Kojève, Alexandre, 20, 23, 153

Lacan, Jacques, 2, 3, 6–33, 47, 48, 102, 103, 107, 111, 112, 134, 152, 153, 154, 162, 163
lack (Lacan), 25, 28
Language, 3, 4, 7, 9, 10, 11, 12, 13, 27, 28, 30, 31, 35, 36, 37, 47, 50, 51, 52, 54, 57, 59, 61, 107, 118, 119–20, 134, 144
Lévi-Strauss, Claude, 1, 2, 10, 31, 43, 44, 152
literature, 51, 59, 143
logocentrism, 39, 40, 41, 44, 45, 48, 60
love, 16, 24, 25, 26, 28, 33, 114
Lukács, Georg, 136–8, 146, 158
Lyotard, Jean-François, 5, 96, 106–8, 117–25, 131–3, 134, 138–40, 158, 159, 160, 166

madness, 8, 65, 66, 67, 68, 69, 72, 83, 102–3
Mandel, Ernest, 145, 161
Marcuse, Herbert, 127, 160
Marx, Karl, 3, 6, 54, 61, 78, 81, 86, 94–5, 96, 98, 99, 101, 105, 107, 109, 110, 113, 132, 141, 167
Marxism, 1, 2, 3, 33, 60, 61, 85, 86–8, 94, 99, 100, 101, 106, 107, 109, 110, 113, 115, 116, 123, 132, 135, 139, 141, 142, 144, 145, 147
master and slave, 16, 20, 21, 22, 24
master narratives, 100, 131, 132–3, 139, 141, 142
May '68, 6, 7, 106, 107, 110, 113, 115

metaphor and metonymy, 11, 13, 18, 46, 47, 50, 51, 52, 53, 54, 55, 57, 148, 155
mirror phase, 10, 15, 27, 29, 30
modernization, 70, 148
montage, 135

narratives, 120–1, 122–3, 132, 133, 141–2
nature–culture, 18, 41, 42, 44, 48
need, 24, 25
'new philosophers', 109, 111–16, 131
Nietzsche, Friedrich, 4, 5, 49, 50, 51, 58, 61, 63, 65, 73, 76, 81, 83, 93, 96–8, 108, 115, 116, 139, 149, 155, 166
Norris, Christopher, 61, 156, 163, 164

Oedipus complex, 10, 19, 27, 28, 30, 101
Panopticon, 75, 76, 83, 89
pastiche, 133, 144–5
phallus, 19, 28, 29, 30, 31, 32, 33
phenomenology, 7, 38, 48, 106
phonocentrism, 38, 40, 41, 44
Plato, 26, 51, 58
postmodernism, 117–40, 144
Poulantzas, Nicos, 91, 92, 157, 158
power, 71, 73, 74, 77, 78, 80–3, 86–7, 90–4, 101, 106, 111, 112, 113, 115, 118, 124, 149, 165

real (Lacan), 31
Rée, Jonathan, 155
Reich, Wilhelm, 79, 100, 154

Rousseau, Jean-Jacques, 42, 44

Sartre, Jean-Paul, 1, 2, 15, 16, 111, 153
Saussure, Ferdinand de, 3, 8, 12, 35, 39, 44, 45, 152
schizophrenia, 99–100, 102, 103, 104, 134, 145
sexuality, 78–80, 157, 161
Soper, Kate, 157
sous-rature (Derrida), 35, 41, 49, 56
state, 69, 86–7, 91, 92, 93, 97, 100, 101, 109, 110, 113, 115, 116, 118, 122, 123
structuralism, 1, 2, 3, 7, 43, 80, 142, 143
supplement (Derrida), 42
Surrealists, 128–9
surveillance, 73, 74, 75, 80, 84
symbolic (Lacan), 27, 28, 29, 30, 102

technical rationality, 76, 92, 156
time, 53, 55, 133–4, 146
totality, 86, 111, 122, 134, 138, 143, 161
trace (Derrida), 36

unconscious, the, 9, 11, 13, 17, 18, 31, 47, 48, 51, 100, 101, 142, 146

Weber, Max, 76–7
will to power, 51, 96, 98, 101, 104
Winnicott, D. W., 14, 153
Wittgenstein, Ludwig, 119, 159, 164
writing, 38, 39, 41, 42, 43, 44, 45, 46, 48, 49, 58, 155